Communication

Communication Skills: The Definitive Guide to Effectively Improving Your Social Skills, Boundaries, Mind Control and Public Speaking

By

Salma Stockdale

Table of Contents

Chapter 1:
What Are Emotions?

What Exactly Is An Emotion?

The scientific answer to that would be that an emotional is a psychological state that has three different components: the subjective experience, a physical response, and a behavioral or expressive response.

There are many different ways psychologists have tried to come up with in order to explain emotions. In 1972, a psychologist by the name of Paul Eckman proposed there are six, basic human emotions that are universal. Those emotions include disgust, fear, anger, happiness, surprise and sadness. In 1999, he expanded that list to include excitement, embarrassment, shame, contempt, pride, amusement, and satisfaction.

In between Eckman's times, in the 1980's, Robert Plutchik suggested another classification system. This system was called the wheel of emotions. He suggested there are different emotions that can be combined with one another in order to create another emotion, just like an artist might mix together the primary colors to make another color. Plutchik proposes there are eight primary emotions: happiness, sadness, anger, fear, trust, disgust, surprise, and anticipation. When they are combined, they create another emotion. For example, when happiness and anticipation are combined, they may make excitement.

So what about the three different components of emotions? This may better help you understand your own.

Subjective Experience

Emotions are subjective even though all humans experience the basic, universal emotions. Regardless of our backgrounds or our cultures, we all experience the same basic emotions such as anger, sadness, or happiness. However, our experience of these emotions is actually unique. For example, not all anger is the same. There are subcategories of anger such as mild annoyance all the way up to blinding range.

We never seem to experience a pure form of each emotion, either. Mixed emotions over an even tor a situation your life is not uncommon. Those who are faced with a new job might feel both excited and nervous. Those who are having children or getting married might have anything from joy to anxiety, to all the emotions in between. They can happen at the same time or they may happen one after the other.

Physical Response

You've most likely felt your stomach lurch or twist when you're anxious or your heart palpate with fear. This is a physical response to your emotions. Many of these responses can include sweaty palms, a racing heart, and rapid breathing. These are all part of the sympathetic nervous system, which a branch of the autonomic nervous system. This part of your nervous system controls the body's fight or flight response, and when faced with a threat, these responses prepare your body to flee or face a threat.

Early studies of the physical forms of emotion focused on autonomic response, recent research has targeted the brain's role in your emotions. Brain scans show that the amygdala, a part of your limbic system, has a role in your emotions, especially fear. This is a tiny, almond shaped component of the brain that has been linked to hunger and thirst, as well as emotion and memory.

Behavioral Response

This final component is most likely the one you are most familiar with, the expression of emotions. We spend a lot of time interpreting emotional expressions of those around us, and our ability to accurately understand the expressions of their emotions is what gives us emotional intelligence. These expressions play a large role in our body language. Expressions such as smiling or frowning are universal across the globe.

Our culture also plays a large role in how we express emotions. For example, in Japan, those who are in the presence of an authority figure mask their fear or disgust. They almost seem to shut-down.

Emotions vs. Moods

Did you know that your emotions and moods are actually different? An emotion is something that is short-lived and intense, and they're likely to have a definite and identifiable cause. For example, you may feel angry after an argument with a friend or lover.

A mood is a milder version of an emotion that is longer-lasting. It's usually hard to determine the specific cause of a mood. For example, you may feel sad or lonely for several days without a real reason to feel that way.

Emotions Can Motivate Us to Take Action

Let's say you're facing an exam in the morning that you know is going to be very difficult. What motivates you to study in order to pass that exam? The fear or anxiety you're feeling of failing that important exam. You experienced motivation due to your emotions.

People usually take action in order to experience a positive emotion and minimize their risk of feeling a negative emotion. For example, a person might try to find social activities or hobbies that leave them feel content, happy, and excited. They may also avoid a situation that could lead to sadness, boredom, or anxiety.

Emotions Help Us Survive, Thrive, and Avoid Danger

Darwin believed that emotions were adaptations we developed in order to survive and reproduce. Anger made us confront the source of our irritation, and fear made us flee the threat. Love helped us find mates and seek out reproductions. Emotions are an adaptive role in our lives that motivate us to take action that will maximize chances for success.

Emotions Can Help Us Make Decisions

We may think that our decisions are guided purely by logic and rationality, but our emotions always play a role in our good decision making process. In fact, research on those who have damage to their emotional intelligence shows that they make poor decisions, while those who have good emotional intelligence have excellent decision making skills.

Emotions Allow Other People to Understand Us

Interaction with others is something that happens on a daily basis to us, and it's important that we give them emotional cues to help them understand what we're feeling. These cues can include body language like facial expressions, or stating how we're feeling directly. When we tell someone we're feeling sad, happy, frightened, or excited, we're giving them imperative information that allow them to take action.

Emotions Allow Us to Understand Others

The emotional expression of others around us provides us with a wealth of social information. Communicating socially is an imperative part of our daily lives and relationships, ad when we can interpret and intact with those emotions of others, we're able to build stronger relationships. It allows us to respond in a deeper, more meaningful way that helps us strengthen the bonds with one another.

Darwin was one of the earliest researchers who scientifically studied emotions. He suggested that they are displayed in order for our survival and safety. For example, coming across a hissing or spitting animal tells you the animal is angry and upset. You are more likely to stay away and survive by not getting injured. In addition, we need to be aware of each other's emotions in order to stay out of stressful, dangerous situations and learn how to defuse them successfully.

Chapter 2:
What Is Emotional Intelligence?

What Is Emotional Intelligence?

Your emotional intelligence is your capability to identify, use, understand, and manage your emotions on a positive way to relieve stress, communicate in an effective manner, empathize with those around you, overcome daily challenges, and defuse conflicts. It can impact many different aspects of your life, such as your behavior and how you interact with those around you.

If you have a high emotional intelligence, then you're able to see your emotional state, as well as the emotional state of those around you. You can engage with the people around you and draw them to you rather than push them away. You can use your understanding of their emotions in order to relate to them better, and form healthier relationships. You can also use it to achieve more success at work and lead a more fulfilling life.

Your emotional intelligence has three different attributes. These attributes include:

- Self-awareness: Your ability to see your own emotions and how they're affecting your thoughts, behavior, and actions. It's also your ability to recognize your strengths and weaknesses, and your level of self-confidence.

- Self-manage: This is your ability to control your spontaneous feelings and actions, as well as manage your emotions in a healthy manner. Those who can self-

6

manage can take initiative, complete commitments, and adapt to their circumstances.

- Social awareness: This is your ability to understand the emotions, concerns, and needs of those around you by picking up on their emotional cues, your ability to feel comfortable in a social setting, and how to recognize the dynamics of a group or organization.

Characteristics of Emotional Intelligence

According to Daniel Goleman, there are actually five elements to emotional intelligence. You'll recognize some of these from the previous chapter, but we're going to expand upon them.

Self-awareness

You already know that self-awareness is your ability to understand your own emotions, and that you don't allow your emotions to rule over you. Those who are self-aware are confident individuals because they're able to allow their intuition to take control rather than letting their emotions take control.

Those who have self-awareness first must be able to take an honest look at themselves and know their strengths and weaknesses. They work on those areas in order to perform better.

Most psychologists believe this is the most important part of emotional intelligence.

Self-regulation

When you're able to control your emotions and impulses, you have self-regulation. Those who are able to self-regulate do not allow themselves to become jealous or angry, and they do not ever make carless, impulsive decisions. They are able to think before they act. Some characteristics of this ability to self-regulate include comfort with change, thoughtfulness, integrity, and the ability to say no to others.

Motivation

Motivation plays a key role in having a high degree of emotional intelligence. Those who are motivated are able to defer immediate results for long-term success. They're productive, enjoy a challenge, and are effect in whatever they do.

Empathy

This is considered the second most important part of emotional intelligence. Empathy is your ability to identify with others and understand their needs, wants and viewpoints. Those who have empathy are excellent at recognizing other's feelings, even when they are not obvious. Empathetic people are great at managing relationships, relating to others, and listening. They do not judge quickly and avoid stereotyping others, and they live their lives in an honest and open way.

Social Skills

It's easy to talk with and like people who have excellent social skills, which is another sign of high emotional intelligence. Those who have strong social skills are team players and focus on helping others before they focus on their own success. They manage disputes, communicate effectively, and are masters at relationships.

Why Is Emotional Intelligence So Important?

Emotional intelligence is very important for everyone. We know that those who are the smartest are not always the most successful or the most fulfilled in their lives. We all know someone who is academically brilliant but they're not socially graceful and they're unsuccessful in their work or their personal relationships due to their ineptness. Our intellectual intelligence is not enough for us to be successful and happy in life. Your intellectual intelligence or IQ can get you into college, but your emotional intelligence is what will help you manage your emotions and the stress when you're facing final exams.

So what areas of your life does emotional intelligence affect?

- Work: Your emotional intelligence affects your work life significantly. If you have a high emotional intelligence, you can navigate the social complexities of your workplace and lead or motivate others. You can excel in your career. When it comes to gauging job candidates, companies view emotional intelligence as more important than technical ability and require emotional intelligence testing before they hire candidates.

- Physical Health: Chronic stress is a serious condition for those who are unable to manage their emotions. It leads to some serious health complications such as raised blood pressure, a suppressed immune system, an increased risk of heart attack and stroke, infertility, and a speed up of the aging process. Your first step is going

9

to be learning how to relieve stress if you have a low emotional intelligence, but we'll get to that in later chapters.

- Mental Health: Chronic stress is also very detrimental to your mental health, and makes you vulnerable to illnesses such as anxiety and depression. If you're unable to manage or understand emotions, then you won't be able to manage mood swings. This can lead to the inability to form or manage strong relationships, and this leads to you feeling lonely and isolated.

- Relationships: If you have a stronger emotional intelligence level, then you are able to forge strong relationships with those around you because you can control your emotions and gauge the emotions of those you're speaking with or just being with. This can help you both in your personal and work life.

Chapter 3:
Emotional and Mental Intelligence

What Is Mental Health Or Emotional Health?

Your emotional and mental health refers to your psychological well-being. It includes the quality of your relationships, how you feel about yourself, and your ability to manage your emotions and deal with difficulties in a calm manner.

A good mental health is not just about the absence of mental health problems. It's about being free from anxiety, depression, and other psychological issues. Mental and emotional health refer to positive characteristics. Remember that feeling bad is not the same as feeling good, and while some people may not have negative feelings, they need to do things that make them feel positive in order to feel mental and emotional health.

Those who are mentally and emotionally healthy have:

- A zest for life, laughing and fun.

- A sense of contentment.

- The ability to handle stress and brush past adversity.

- A sense of meaning in their relationships and activities.

- The flexibility to adapt to change and learn new things.

- A balance between their work life, play life, rest, activity, etc.

- The ability to create and maintain a fulfilling relationship with themselves and others.

- High self-esteem and self-confidence.

When you harbor these characteristics of mental and emotional health and stability, you're able to participate in life to the fullest by being productive and having meaningful activities and relationships. When you have these characteristics, you're able to weather life's challenges and stressful moments.

The Role of Resilience in Mental and Emotional Health

When you are emotionally and mentally healthy, it doesn't mean that you don't go through some bad times in your life or experience some emotional problems. Everyone goes through loss, disappointments, and change. They're all normal parts of life that cause anxiety, sadness, and stress.

However, those who have a healthy emotional outlook are able to deal with those moments and bounce back from the trauma, adversity, and stress. This is known as resilience.

People who have tools for coping with those difficult situations and maintain a positive outlook are able to stay focused, creative, and flexible during the bad times, as well as the good.

As aforementioned, one of the key components to having a healthy emotional outlook is being able to balance your stress and your emotions. Your ability to recognize and express your emotions appropriately will help you avoid becoming tuck in anxiety, depression and other negative mood states. You also have to have a strong support network. Being able to trust people and having them around you turns you toward encouragement, which boosts your resilience during those tough times.

Physical Health Is Connected To Mental and Emotional Health

Your body's needs should be of your first concern when it comes to your emotional and mental health. Your mind and your body are linked in a powerful way, and when you improve your physical well-being, you will experience a greater mental and emotional well-being. Exercise strengthens your heart and lungs, and it also releases endorphins that energize and lift your mood.

The activities you perform on a daily basis affect the way you feel emotionally and physically.

Here are some ways to improve your physical health:

- Get rest. When you get enough sleep, seven to eight hours every night, you're able to function with a more clear-headed mind. Without enough sleep, you can develop a short fuse which leads to outbursts.

- Learn about nutrition and practice it. First, do some research on what you should be eating and things you might want to avoid, like excess sugar and processed foods. Then, keep a diary of what you eat on a daily basis and how you feel after you eat those foods for a week. You'll start to see patterns as to what foods might aggravate you and what foods help you stay focused and alert.

- Exercise in order to relieve stress. You don't have to go to a gym in order to boost your endorphins and make yourself mentally happier and healthier. Just take the stairs instead of the elevator or take a walk at lunch for fifteen minutes. Instead of taking the first bus stop, walk to the second one. There are many ways you can add exercise into your daily routine.

- Get some sunlight. You should have ten to fifteen minutes of direct sunlight every day. You can do this while gardening, exercising, or even socializing.

- Limit your alcohol and drug consumption. This includes cigarettes. All of these are stimulants that make you feel good for the short term, but they have some long-term negative side effects for not only your body, but your emotional and mental health, too.

Improve Mental and Emotional Health by Taking Care of Yourself

If you want to maintain and strengthen your emotional and mental health, you have to pay attention to your needs and feelings first. Do not allow stress and negative emotions to build up, but instead try to maintain a balance between your daily responsibilities and the things that make you happy. If you take care of your needs first, you'll be able to deal with challenges when they arise in a much more positive manner.

Taking care of you includes some of the following:

- Do things that positively impact others. When you're being useful to others and being valued for what you're doing, you're building your self-esteem and self-confidence.

- Practice self-discipline. When you practice self-control, this leads to a sense of hopefulness and help you overcome despair.

- Learn to discover something new. Think of discovering something new as intellectual candy. Join a book club, take an adult educational class, learn a new language, visit a museum, or travel somewhere new, even if it's just a town in the same county you live in.

- Enjoy the beauty of art or nature. Studies have shown that those who take the time to smell the roses and view nature are able to lower their blood pressure and reduce their stress. Just sitting on the beach can be a great way to relax your nerves.

- Manage your stress. Stress is our enemy. It used to be necessary for short bursts of time to survive in the wild, but we're not chronically stressed, which can lead to heart disease and many other nasty illnesses. Try taking some stress management classes or utilizing some of the stress relieving tips found later in this book.

- Limit unhealthy habits such as worrying. Stop becoming absorbed in repetitive mental habits, such as negative thoughts about yourself and the world. These drain your energy, suck up your time, and trigger feelings of fear, anxiety, and depression.

- Appeal to your senses. Be sure to remain calm and energized by appealing to your five senses. Listen to music, put some flower on your desk, massages your hands, or drink a warm cup of tea or hot cocoa. Indulge yourself!

- Engage in creative, meaningful work. When you do something that challenges your creativity and makes you feel productive, you boost your confidence and esteem levels. Try something such as writing, gardening, drawing, building something or playing an instrument.

- Get a pet. You're right, they're a big responsibility, but caring for one makes you feel loved and needed. Pets give you unconditional love and they don't care about who you fought with that day or whether or not you forgot the milk. They're always waiting for you when you get home and they're never in a bad mood.

- Make leisure time a priority. Play-time for adults is just as much a necessity as it is for children. We need to engage in leisure time in order to unwind from a hard day at work.

- Make some time for appreciation and contemplation. Think about everything you're grateful for and take some time to meditate, enjoy the sunset, or take a moment to pay attention to what's positive, good and beautiful throughout your day.

Remember that everyone is different and not everything that is good and beneficial to you will be the same for others. Some feel better when they're relaxing while others need stimulation and excitement in order to feel better. Just find the activities in your life that make you feel boosted and energized.

Risk Factors for Mental and Emotional Problems

Mental and emotional health is shaped by experiences. Your early childhood experiences and memories are very significant. Genetic and biological factors may also play a role, but these are usually shaped and changed by experiences, too.

There are some risk factors that are able to compromise your mental and emotional health. These factors include:

- A poor connection or attachment with a primary caretaker in early life. If you felt abused, lonely, isolated, unsafe, or confused as an infant or as a young child, you are at a higher risk for mental and emotional complications.

- Traumas or serious loss, especially earl in life. These might include experiencing a war, hospitalization, or even losing a loved one such as a parent or grandparent.

- Learned helplessness. Sometimes people experience negative experiences that lead to a belief that they're helpless and do not have any control over situations in their life.

- Illness. Chronic or disabling illness that isolates children from others can cause emotional and mental distress.

- Medication side-effects. Those who are older who are taking many medications are more at risk for experiencing side-effects, which can lead to emotional distress.

- Substance abuse. Abusing alcohol and drugs can cause mental, physical, and emotional problems.

Whether you've had internal or external factors that shaped your mental and emotional health, it's not too late to make the necessary changes in order to improve your psychological well-being. These risk factors can be counteracted with protective factors such as a healthy lifestyle, strong relationships, and coping strategies that help you manage stress and your negative emotions.

When to Seek Professional Help for Emotional Problems

Sometimes, no matter how hard we try to do it alone, we need a professional to help us with our mental and emotional health. There's no shame in asking for help, and taking that leap will help you improve greatly.

Some red flag emotions and behaviors include:

- Insomnia

- Feeling helpless and hopeless consistently.

- Having problems concentrating at work and at home.

- Using food, nicotine, drugs, or alcohol in order to cope with your emotions.

- Self-destructive or negative thoughts or fears that you can't seem to control.

- Thoughts of suicide or death.

If you have any of these red flags, then it's best that you seek immediate treatment from a professional.

Chapter 4:
Developing Emotional Intelligence

Do you have emotional intelligence? The truth is that everyone has some level of what is referred to as emotional intelligence – some people just have more of it than others. If you are lacking emotional intelligence, luckily you can learn to develop more of it and use it in your everyday life. But first, how do you know whether you have a lot of emotional intelligence, or only a little? In order to answer this, you will first have to understand what emotional intelligence is.

Emotional intelligence is all about being able to know what people around you are feeling – what their emotions are. People with high emotional intelligence can easily tell what people they are associating with are feeling, and can then use it to benefit both themselves and others. If you understand what others are feeling, you will know how to treat them, talk to them, successfully work with them, and so much more.

You are probably wondering how you can develop your emotional intelligence. Well, you need to try to be more aware of your surroundings. Next time you are around others, try to take in all the little things about them that can signify what they are feeling. Are you someone who is generally caught up in a million things at once? Are you often stressed, worried, and frazzled? If this sounds like you, then you might be having trouble developing emotional intelligence because you don't take the time to focus on what is going on around you - you are always caught up in other things.

To develop your emotional intelligence, try practicing mindfulness. Mindfulness is just focusing on the present – instead of what might happen in the future or what has happened in the past. It sounds so simple, doesn't it? However, the truth is that with all the distractions of life, putting it into practice can be another story entirely.

You will have to work at it – so don't be discouraged if at first you fail. Practice again and again, and you will find yourself getting better at truly living in the present moment. In order to practice mindfulness, it is essential to be calm. So, you may need to do some breathing exercises to get rid of any stress or anxiety. This will hopefully allow you to be calm enough to focus on only what is going on around you, instead of worrying needlessly about other things.

How will this new skill called mindfulness help you develop your emotional intelligence? Well, if you practice mindfulness when you are around others, you will be able to easily pick up on their emotions. You will be focused on the present, which make you a lot less likely to miss a sudden change in, for example, someone's face or voice. It is the little signs like these that can tell you how someone is feeling – and in order to notice them, you need to be completely focused on what is going on around you.

Hopefully these tips will help you develop more emotional intelligence in no time. To quickly summarize the key points of this chapter, be sure to remember how important it is to get rid of stress so you can focus on the present. This will increase your emotional intelligence greatly. But, now that you have greater emotional intelligence, you need to learn how to apply it in everyday life. If correctly applied, emotional intelligence can be extremely helpful. Keep reading to learn how to apply emotional intelligence in your life. Emotional intelligence can help you develop and sustain the relationships you have always wanted. With emotional intelligence, you will have more control over the relationships in your life. If you want to improve a relationship that you feel needs work, you will be able to. If you want to mend a friendship, it won't be as hard. Your family and work life will greatly benefit from your new skill – so don't wait any longer! The next chapter of this book will help you on your journey to improving the relationships in your life.

Chapter 5:
Applying Emotional Intelligence

In the last chapter you learned how to develop more emotional intelligence. Hopefully you are starting to apply these tips and ideas in your own life – but you may be having some trouble with that. Maybe you don't know exactly how to apply emotional intelligence to you everyday life. Well, applying emotional intelligence is just about learning how to use it to help you develop and grow relationships to their full potential.

To apply your newly developed emotional intelligence, you will need to first think about the situations that it will be useful in. So, think about this: are there any relationships in your life that you need to improve and work on? Is there any area in your life where you are having trouble with relationships: whether this may be personal or professional? The first step to developing these relationships is recognizing what situations require emotional intelligence, and what situations require you to use more emotional intelligence than others.

So, think about the situations that you encounter in day to day life which could be made easier if you were to simply apply some emotional intelligence. What interactions with others are difficult? What relationships are faltering or even falling apart? Now you know where to apply emotional intelligence. The next step is to know how to apply it to the specific situation.

In order to apply emotional intelligence, you will need to recognize these situations and then remember to take others' emotions into consideration when you are in these specific situations. Some situations will call for more emotional intelligence than others. These are situations where you are really struggling – but with emotional intelligence, you will find a way to work out these problems in no time at all.

For example, if you are always arguing with someone, and can sense your relationship with them is gradually deteriorating, this is a situation where emotional intelligence can be a great help. With emotional intelligence, you can take the steps to gradually mend your relationship and become a happier, healthier person as a result.

First, take a step back from the situation and think about how you can apply emotional intelligence for the benefit of the relationship. Then, try to really focus on understanding what the other person is feeling and going through. Try as hard as you can to read their subtle voice tones, body language, reactions, and anything else, so you can figure out what emotions they are experiencing.

So, what do you do once you have some sort of idea of their emotions? The next step is to use this new knowledge to treat them accordingly, talk to them in a way that is best considering what their emotion is at the moment, and just interact with them in a way that takes their emotions into consideration. So, for example, if they seem to be having a very hard day, you would talk to them in a tone that might make them feel better. Of course, this is only one example – you will have to figure out how to apply your emotional intelligence to the specific situations that have occurred or will occur in your everyday life.

My hope is that now that you know more about how to apply emotional intelligence, you will find ways to strengthen the relationships in your life and build new ones that you never would have been able to build before. Between the information from this chapter and the information included in the last, you already know a lot about emotional intelligence and how you can use it in terms of relationships.

In the next two chapters, we will get more specific and delve into two particular categories of relationships. This will help you to learn about situations on a more specific and case by case level – but of course, in the end you will still have to tailor all of this knowledge to fit your own unique circumstances.

The next chapter will focus on how you can use emotional intelligence in your personal relationships. You will learn how you can start helping these relationships right now by simply applying the emotional intelligence that you have developed. In this chapter, the focus will be specifically on family relationships. This will include relationships with both members of your immediate family and your extended family.

Chapter 6:
Raising Emotional Intelligence

How to Raise Your Emotional Intelligence

So you know that you have a low emotional intelligence, but how do you boost it?

The information around use comes to the brain from our senses, and when that information becomes overwhelming or stressful to use, instinct takes over and we act with fight, flight or freeze. In order to have access to a wider range of choices and the ability to make good decisions, we have to be able to bring our emotions into balance when we need to.

Our memories are strongly linked to our emotions, and when we learn to stay connected to the emotional part of our brain at the same time we're connected to the rational part, we're expanding our range of choices and factoring emotional memory into our decision-making processes. This helps you stop continually repeating earlier mistakes.

In order to improve emotional intelligence and decision-making abilities, you have to first understand your emotions. Then you have to manage them. This can be accomplished through practicing and maintaining key skills that help you control and manage the overwhelming stress of everyday life, and helps you become an effective communicator.

You can develop emotional intelligence using a few key skills.

Emotional intelligence can be built by lowering stress levels, remaining focused, and becoming and staying connected to those around you and yourself. You can do this through a few key skills. The first two are imperative for controlling and managing your stress and the last three will improve your communication with others. Each skill it built upon the last skill, so you must start with the first one and work your way down.

These skills include:

- Reducing stress in stressful situations.

- Recognizing emotions and keeping them from overwhelming you.

- Connecting emotionally with those around you with nonverbal communication.

- Using humor in order to stay connected, even in a challenging situation.

- Resolving conflict through positivity and confidence.

You can learn these key skills at any time, but there is a different between learning about emotional intelligence and applying it to your life. Knowing that you ought to do something doesn't mean you will, and it's especially difficult when you've become overwhelmed by stress.

In order to permanently change your behavior and stand up under pressure, you have to learn how to overcome the stress in the moment and the stress in your relationships by knowing when your partner is feeling stressed. This means that you can't just read about it in order to master it. You have to practice the everyday skills in your life.

So here are the steps to reducing your emotional stress and building your emotional intelligence.

Reduce Stress in the Moment

High levels of stress can really overwhelm your mind and body, and they get in the way of your ability to accurately understand a situation. You lose the ability to hear what others are saying, what they're feeling or might need, and how to communicate in a clear and concise manner.

When you learn how to calm yourself down and relieve that stress in a stressful moment, you learn how to stay balanced, focused, and in control no matter what challenge you may be facing.

Try the following three steps in order to rid yourself of stress in the moment:

1. Realize that you're stressed. I know it may seem silly, but sometimes we don't understand that we're actually stressed out. We don't know the warning signs that stress is overwhelming us, like a quickened heart rate, increased breathing, muscles tensing, stomach being tight or sore, hands clenching, or even tears of frustration. Being aware of your physical responses allows you to regulate the tension as it is occurring.

2. Identify your stress response. Each person reacts in a different way to stress, and if you tend to become angry or agitated under stress, you're going to need different techniques than someone who becomes withdrawn or depressed. Those who become angry need quieting activities while those who become withdrawn or depressed need stimulating activities. If you freeze up, you may need to speed up in some ways and slow down in others.

3. Discover the techniques that work best for you. The best way you can reduce stress in the moment and rapidly is by engaging one of your senses such as sight, smell, sound, taste, or touch. People respond differently to sensory input, so you have to find the ones that are soothing or energizing to you. If you're a visual person, you might try surrounding yourself with uplifting photos, or if you respond to sound, you might want to try a wind chime to reduce stress levels. Each person is different, so you have to explore your needs emotionally in order to figure out what will work best for you.

Develop Emotional Awareness

When you are able to connect to your emotions and have a moment-to-moment awareness of what those emotions are and how they're affecting your thoughts and actions, you are able to understand yourself and remain calm and focused in a tense situation with someone else.

There are many of us who are disconnected from our emotions, especially the core ones such as sadness, anger, joy, and fear. This can be a result of a negative childhood event that taught to us keep our emotions hidden and to shut them off. We may be able to deny, distort, and numb our feelings, but we cannot seem to eliminate them, so we must know how to deal with them. They're still present in our everyday lives and without emotional awareness, we cannot understand our motivations and needs, or communicate them with others. We're at a far greater risk of becoming overwhelmed in a situation that may appear threatening.

In order to understand your emotions, you must first identify with kind of relationship you have with them.

- Do you have feelings that flow, coming across one emotion to the next as your experiences change throughout the day?

- Are your emotions coupled with physical sensations that you experience in areas such as your chest or stomach?

- Do you experience discrete emotions and feelings like sadness, anger, joy, and fear with subtle facial expressions?

- Do you experience intense emotions that capture both the attention of others and your attention?

- Do you ignore your emotions or do they play a role in your decision-making process?

If you do not experience any of these, then you may have tamped down or turned off your emotions. If you want to become emotionally intelligent and healthy, then you have to reconnect to those core emotions and accept them, even become comfortable with them.

When developing emotional awareness, you first have to learn how to deal with stress. If you haven't learned how to manage that, then you won't be able to control any of your emotions or even acknowledge them.

Nonverbal Communication

Not only do we need excellent communication skills verbally, but we also need nonverbal communication skills in order to manage our stress and recognize the stress of others. Remember that what you're saying is usually less important than how you're saying it, and the other nonverbal gestures you make, how you're sitting, how fast or loud you're talking, how close you're standing, or the amount of eye contact you're making with the other person all tell them how you're feeling, as well as how they're feeling.

If you want to hold the attention and build a connection with others, then you have to be aware of your nonverbal communication or body language. You have to be able to easily read and respond to their nonverbal cues, too.

Even when we're silent, we have the capability of still sending communication to another person. Think about what you're transmitting, as well as what you're feeling from that person. If you clench your teeth and tell someone you're okay or fine, they're going to know that you're not find or okay. Our nonverbal messages can transmit trust, interest, desire, and excitement or confusion, distrust, fear, and disinterest.

So how can you improve your nonverbal communication?

Well, when you're communicating nonverbally in a successful manner, you're able to manage your stress and recognize the emotions you're feeling, as well as understand the signals you send and receive to and from others. When you're communicating with someone else:

- Focus on that person. If you're not completely focused on that person and instead thinking about what you're going to say or if you're daydreaming, then you will miss many nonverbal cues in your conversation.

- Make eye contact. This communicates interest, and helps maintain the flow of a conversation. It also helps you gauge the other person's response.

- Pay attention to nonverbal cues. Are you sending mixed facial expressions or perhaps using a tone of voice that's completely different than what you want the other person to gather from the situation? Pay attention to your posture and your touch, as well as your gestures. What is the timing and the pace of the conversation? All of these are very important.

Use Humor

Laughter and humor are all natural antidotes to life's daily stress because they lighten up our burdens and help use keep things in perspective. A natural, hearty laugh can reduce your stress levels, elevate your mood, and bring your nervous system into balance.

When you playfully communicate, you:

- Take hardships in stride. You are able to view your frustrations and disappointments from a new perspective and you can survive some everyday annoyances. Laughter also helps you survive the hard times and the setbacks. That's why you see people who are trying to make others laugh after a funeral or after a particularly bad argument. They're attempting to 'lighten the mood'.

- Smooth over differences. We're all different and that means we all have different opinions. Rather than let these opinions and differences upset us, we should use laughter to help us say things that might be difficult to express without causing a fight.

- Simultaneously relax and energize. Communicating in a playful manner helps us relieve fatigue and relax our bodies, allowing us to recharge and accomplish more.

- Become more creative. Laughter helps us loosen up and free ourselves from rigid ways of thinking and being. This allows us to become more creative and see things in a new way.

So how do you develop playful communication?

- Set aside some regular, quality playtime such as joking, playing or laughing. The more you do it, the easier it becomes.

- Find activities that are enjoyable that loosen you up and help you to embrace that playful side of yourself.

- Practice with babies, animals, young children, and outgoing people who enjoy playful banter themselves.

Resolve Conflict in a Positive Manner

Disagreements and arguments happen in every relationship because two people never have the same opinions, needs, and expectations at the same time. That doesn't have to be a bad thing, though. Resolving your conflicts in a healthy way strengthens the trust between two people because when it's not perceived as a threatening or punishing event, it grows creativity, freedom, and safety.

Managing conflict in a positive, trust-building way is supported by the previous four skills. When you know how to manage stress, become emotionally present and aware, communicate in a nonverbal manner, and use humor and play to distress a situation, you're more equipped to handle an emotionally charged event and defuse many issues before they even escalate.

Here are a few ways you can start resolving conflicts in a trust-building way:

- Stay focused on the present. When you're letting go of old hurts and resentments, you're able to recognize the reality of a current situation and view it in a different light. You view it as a new opportunity to resolve old feelings about conflicts.

- Choose your arguments. Arguments waste a lot of time and energy, especially if they're not resolved in a positive way. Consider what you really believe is worth arguing about and what isn't.

- Forgive. It's a lot easier said than done, I know, but forgiveness is not only for the one who hurt you, but for you. Stop looking to punish or seek revenge on those who hurt you because it's only going to take away from your life.

- End the conflicts that aren't able to be resolved. It takes two in order to be in love, and it takes two for an argument to continue. You are able to step away from an argument and disengage yourself, even if you do not agree with the other person. Sometimes it's just not something that can be resolved right away.

Observation

You should observe how you're reacting to people. Do you rush to judging them before you know all the facts? Are you someone who sees stereotypes? Be honest about how you think and react to others, and try putting yourself in their place. Be more open about their perspectives and their needs.

Work Environment

Do you always seek out attention for accomplishments? Humility is an excellent quality of those who have emotional intelligence. They don't need reassurance from others that they are doing the right thing. It doesn't mean that you lack self-confidence or are shy if you don't want too much recognition. It just means that you realize you're not the most important person on this planet. It's best to give others a chance to shine and focus on them, and stop worrying so much about obtaining praise yourself.

Self-Evaluation

Know your weaknesses and accept that you're not a perfect person, and that you are able to work on some of those areas in your life in order to be a better person. Be honest about this with yourself because it can really change your life.

Examine your Reactions

How do you react in a stressful situation? Are you upset and angry every time something doesn't go your way? Do you blame others are show anger toward them when it's not their fault? Your ability to stay calm and in control during a difficult situation is valued in both the business world and outside of it. Keep your emotions under control and learn how to reduce stress in the moment.

Take Responsibility

When you take responsibility for your actions and apologize to someone directly when you've hurt their feelings or done something wrong, they are more likely to move on and make things right. Be honest with them and sincere about your apology, or it will come across as flat and unwelcoming.

Examine Your Effect on Others

Before you even take an action, examine in your mind how that action will affect those around you. If your decision is going to impact someone else, put yourself in their place. How are they going to feel about this action? Would you want to experience what they're going to experience? If you have to take the action, how can you help them deal with the effects?

Supportive Relationships

It doesn't matter how much time and effort you put into improving your emotional and mental health, you still need others company in order to feel your best. Humans are social and have an emotional need for relationships and a positive connection with someone else. We are not meant to thrive in isolation. We have a social brain that craves companionship, even if the experience for us is shy and distrustful.

When you socially interact with others, you can reduce your stress levels. The key is to find a relationship with someone who is a good listener and supportive of you. You need someone who you can talk to on a regular basis, face-to-face, who will listen to you without having an agenda or telling you how you ought to think or feel. A good listener listens to the emotions behind the words and doesn't interrupt or criticize the other person. The best way to find a good listener is to be one yourself.

Here are a few tips you can use in order to connect with others:

- Get away from the television or the computer screen. These instruments have their place in our lives, but they do not have the same effect as a real expression of interest or a reassuring touch. Communication is a nonverbal experience that requires being in direct contact with others, so never neglect real world interactions.

- Spend time with people you like on a daily basis, face-to-face. Spending time with others that you enjoy helps you relax and get rid of stress. Make time for friends, colleagues, neighbors, and family members that are positive, upbeat and interested in what you're doing. Take time to inquire about the people you meet on a daily basis.

- Volunteer. Not only does volunteering have a positive effect on how you feel about yourself, it has a beneficial effect on the others around you. The meaning and purpose you will find in helping out others will help you feel enriched and expand your horizons. There are no limits when it comes to volunteering. You can volunteer at schools, nonprofits, charitable organizations, churches, and animal shelters.

- Be a joiner. Join in on social action, networking, conversation, and interest groups that meet on a regular basis. This offers wonderful opportunities for you to find others with common interests who could be potential friends.

Chapter 7:
Emotional Intelligence and Personal Relationships

In order to have the best kind of relationships in your life, you need emotional intelligence. In the past chapters you learned what emotional intelligence is and in general how it can be applied. In this chapter, you will learn specifically how you can apply it to benefit the relationships that you have in your personal life.

I am going to start broadly and talk about extended family. First, you will learn how to use emotional intelligence to take control of relationships with people you may not see as often. So, have you been having trouble with your relationship with, for example, your grandmother or mother? Or are you having trouble relating to your brother-in-law or brother who lives across the country – or maybe even across the world? How can you start to mend these relationships so that you can finally have the kind of interaction with these people that you have dreamed of for so long?

Well, the answer is quite simple. It is emotional intelligence: with emotional intelligence you can take control of these family relationships, so that everyone will be happier. There is no need to continue living full of stress, worry, and feelings of sadness because these relationships just did not work out. If you want to get closer to these people in your life, now you can!

First, figure out what relationships in your life you would like to work on. Think about which relationships are leaving you feeling unhappy because they have not worked out. Figure out which relationships could help you to be a happier person if they were different. Then, act on your wish to mend these relationships. You can just start with one relationship if you do not want to take on too much at one time.

Next, start reaching out to the person that you want to build your relationship with. If you are already planning to see them, don't stress out or worry – even if this is what you normally do. When you see them, or when you talk to them over the phone, try to gauge their emotions. Try to be aware of what they are feeling, and how they are reacting to what you are saying to them – even to just seeing you in general. Your words, actions, and reactions should all depend on how you see them behaving. The way they behave is a great way to tell what they are feeling inside. If you are experienced at reading people's emotions, you will be able to easily figure out how they are feeling and then use this knowledge to both of your benefits. They will benefit from your emotional intelligence as well. Since you are using emotional intelligence, you will be less likely to have a misunderstanding, or say something to them that they will interpret in the wrong way. And, even better, you will be more likely to meet and talk again soon. With emotional intelligence, you are well on your way to building a stronger, healthier relationship with this family member – even if you feel like you don't know them that well because you don't see them every day (or even every year).

The truth is that extended family relationships can be hard to maintain for these very reasons – you just don't know them as well as your other family members. For this reason, it is especially important that all your attention and focus in on them during those few hours each month, or maybe each year, that you get to spend with them. In our busy lives, it is far too often that our attention is elsewhere – making it possible to use emotional intelligence in these situations.

You need to fully focus on the person you are talking to and spending time with, so that you can make up for lost time. Maybe there is something that has happened in their lives since you have last seen them that you don't even know about. Well, the truth is that maybe you are never going to find out about it. Or, at least you are not going to find about all of the details that the people closer to this person know. However, that doesn't mean that you can't read and figure out generalizations about what has gone on from their face, their voice, and their actions – and sometimes, to be honest, that is all you need to know. With this knowledge, you can better understand their actions. It will help you not to lash out at them if you understand the motives for their behavior or harsh words. And it will help you to treat them the way you yourself would want to be treated if you were in their situation – to say the things that will help them through whatever it is that they are going through.

Next, let's think about the relationships with the people you see every day. These relationships encounter plenty of problems of their own. You can build back up a broken relationship by trying to understand what the other person is feeling, and by using this knowledge to interact with them accordingly. For example, take someone who is always fighting with their spouse. In this case, it may be that the two people are not reading each other's emotions correctly. In order to mend the situation, a good first step would be for them to pay attention to the other person's emotions.

In all family relationships, you may have to assess the situation and see if you are focusing on yourself too much. Perhaps you are just wrapped up in worry about your own problems. Or maybe you are worried about what other people think about you. The truth is that in order to have better relationships with these people, you will have to stop focusing on yourself and start focusing on them. You can focus on yourself and them – the interactions you are having together. This will make it harder to misread their face or voice, which is exactly what you want. You want to be able to read them correctly so you know how to act around them and how to talk with them.

Taking control of the personal relationships in your life is all about helping relationships to work so that you can be happy again. It is all about taking your thoughts about what you want the relationships in your life to be like – and making these hopes and dreams become a reality. With a higher emotional intelligence, you can do this easily. In fact, you probably won't believe how easy it is with emotional intelligence.

Right now, you might be thinking that there are other relationships in your life as well – so what about those? These relationships are very different from the relationships that you have with your family. Probably the other largest category of relationships, the one that most people can relate to, are the relationships you have with the people you work with. These professional relationships can be difficult as well – especially if you are in a tough work situation, or a job that you don't really like. But no matter what, knowing how to take control of these professional relationships is very important. In the next chapter, you will learn how emotional intelligence can help you with this.

Chapter 8:
Emotional Intelligence and Professional Relationships

Now you are going to learn how a higher emotional intelligence can help your relationships with your boss and your coworkers. First, let's talk about your boss or supervisor at work. This relationship is obviously very important – and one that you don't want to mess up. Sometimes, this relationship can be very hard – you are trying to act the right way, but one little mistake can send you worrying that your job might be on the line.

So, to prevent this excess worrying, you will need to acquire some emotional intelligence. If you can tell what your boss is thinking and feeling, then even if they aren't saying it you will have a better idea of what is happening. This will prevent you from thinking you are getting fired when in reality they are just having a bad day. It is important to understand people's emotions because these emotions will show in their faces – and you don't want to jump to the wrong conclusion that these emotions are because of you.

Emotional intelligence is all about focusing on what is going on around you – in specific the other people around you and anything about them that could tell you how they are feeling. This is very important in the work situation – there are a lot of people and your ability to interact with them may mean the difference between keeping the job you love and losing it. So how can having more emotional intelligence help you to successfully interact with your coworkers in a way that is both productive and right for the specific job situation you are in? Well, there are so many ways which emotional intelligence can help you interact with coworkers. If you are working as a group with other employees, it is time to make sure you are using your emotional intelligence to the best of your abilities – because you are definitely going to need it.

Prior to this we have basically been talking about relationships where only two people are involved. Now, in the workplace, we are talking about social situations where you are required to work with multiple people – whether this means several people or a whole group. So, what does this mean in terms of using emotional intelligence? Well, unfortunately this means that it is going to be much harder. The reason you will likely find it more difficult is that you simply have more people around you, which means you have more emotions and feelings to try to gauge to the best of your ability.

This just means that it is even more important than before to practice mindfulness and to learn to come to the workplace completely stress-free. If you are not stressed, it will be so much easier to use your emotional intelligence when you are in a group of people. You also need to completely focus on what is going on around you in order to practice emotional intelligence around more than one person. If you have developed these skills which were outlined earlier in the book, it will make it so much easier to work with others. Working with others requires that you understand their emotions because if you can't you either won't know how to interact with them, or, more likely, you will interact with them in the wrong way.

If someone is having a bad day, or something has just happened in your life, then you will need to adjust the way you talk to them accordingly. The failure to do this can result in difficulty working as a group, arguments, or even a fight. However, if you can do this, then the group will work so much more smoothly. Everything will go smoothly because you all are taking the time to understand each other, and to tailor interactions to each specific person depending on the way that person is interacting with you. It is important to be able to look at a person and decide quickly how you should interact with them to achieve the results you want – which in this case is harmony throughout the group which will allow you all to work together and get the job done.

If you are a supervisor at work, whether you are just supervising a small group for a simple project or a larger number of people for a long time, then emotional intelligence is especially important. Without emotional intelligence, how will you ensure that everything with the group is running smoothly? You will get so much work done if you have higher emotional intelligence. Remember, if you don't feel like you currently have a high emotional intelligence, there is no need to fret. Earlier in this book tips were given for how to successfully develop your emotional intelligence. So no matter how lacking you feel that you are in this area, these tips will be just the help that you need. Follow them to have more emotional intelligence in no time – and all the relationships in your life will benefit from it.

In this chapter you learned some tips for using emotional intelligence to help you navigate the difficulties of the workplace. In the last chapter, you learned about using emotional intelligence when at home for the benefit of the relationships that you have there. Now, in the last chapter of the book, we will be talking about emotional intelligence and social skills in general. You will learn how to use your emotional intelligence to have better social skills. So, do you feel that your social skills could use improvement? Well, if you do, then this will be an important section for you. Emotional intelligence will help you to interact with all types of people better.

Chapter 9:
Emotional Intelligence and Social Skills

In the last chapters you have been learning about how to interact with people you know – whether that means close family members or at least people you know of and have seen before. However, that seems to give the impression that emotional intelligence can only be beneficial to relationships you have with people that you already know – however well you may know them. The truth is that emotional intelligence can actually help with any social interaction – even if you don't have an actual relationship with the person and never will. What do I mean by this? Well, let's give some quick examples from everyday life that most people can probably relate to.

If you are, for example, at the store and interacting with a stranger, then emotional intelligence can help. If you are going to see a doctor, emotional intelligence can help. Emotional intelligence can help with all social interactions that you have with anyone, anywhere. If you have emotional intelligence, you can use it to develop your social skills.

So, in what way are you looking to develop your social skills? Are you hoping to have an easier time deciding how to interact with a specific person or type of person? Do you want new social situations to be smoother for you – you want to minimize worrying about them even though they are something you have never experienced before? Or do you want to know what to say in difficult social situations when it seems there are just no words? Well, emotional intelligence can help you in all of these situations.

With emotional intelligence, you will know what to say and how to behave – no matter how foreign the situation is. You will know how to interact with different types of people – and how to decide to interact with someone that you are about to meet. You will also know how to stop worrying about new situations and experiences. How can emotional intelligence help with all of this? Well, it really is simple. As you have already learned, emotional intelligence helps you to tell what other people's emotions are. And in all of these situations, what you really need is to be able to know what the other person is feeling. If you know this, then the interaction will come so much more naturally. Emotional intelligence truly is a wonderful skill to have in these situations!

So, let's start with the first situation and elaborate just a little so that you can get a better idea of this. Is there a specific person that you are having trouble knowing how to interact with? If this is the case, then you can stop worrying about it. Simply use your emotional intelligence when you are in a situation with this person. Try to read their emotions, and interact accordingly. With emotional intelligence, even if you have never met this person before the interaction will still be smooth. Even if you don't get along with this specific type of person, with emotional intelligence, you will be able to make things go better than they normally would. Try to understand them, and think about where they are coming from. Forget everything else you are thinking about, and focus your attention on them, and how you think it would be best to interact with them. This will be sure to help turn an uncomfortable situation into a much more comfortable one.

Next, are you worrying about a social situation because it is new and different? Emotional intelligence will help you to get through even the newest of situations. It is all about being able to learn about the people you are with, even if you have never met them. How do you use emotional intelligence to learn about them? Well, you need to try to read their emotions.

Emotions can be deducted based on how they are speaking, how they look (happy, sad, uncomfortable, nervous) and so much more. If you look closely enough, you can learn about someone you have never met. It is definitely possible – you just have to be focused and you have to be living in the present moment.

Now, let's talk a little about the last scenario that was posed as a question above. This scenario involves difficult social situations when it seems there are no words to say. In a situation like this, it will be extremely important to try to figure out the other person's emotions. Then, you will know what to say based on how they seem to be feeling. All in all, emotional intelligence can really help you with social interaction in so many ways. These were only three examples – there are so many more ways that it can help you. So, this is just another reason to learn how to develop your emotional intelligence.

Part 2: Setting Boundaries

Introduction -What are the everyday boundaries?

Boundaries are the various lines of personal property that help in defining the responsibilities we have, who we really are, and the areas we are limited. A balanced, healthy lifestyle is a product of clearly set out boundaries.

In the modern day life, the need for boundaries has become pertinent to a good living. From home to workplace, the most prominent show of boundary invasion is through the sexual, physical and emotional abuse that runs through the society.

As a parent, it is always necessary setting out the various life boundaries for your family. These are the values you would wish to subscribe to as a family. The boundaries help to indicate the responsibilities of every member of the family and the need to dialog and discuss issues at home. Boundaries at home ensure limits are well set for the right thing: when to begin dating, the mode of dressing, the type of friends to have, bedtime, and physical affection among others.

Setting your everyday life boundaries works to maintain a healthy working relationship at work. As a boss, you will effectively relate with your juniors and vice versa. Everyone understands the role at work. Friends will also learn to appreciate and back each other so long as they have their boundaries.

You must understand the various cases when to do different things. Parents should know their limits and children as well. Everyone in the office should understand their roles. This way, the holistic relationship in the society grows for better.

Worth noting: boundaries start with you. Your limits- your choices!

General Principles

There is dying need to understand the foundations of every boundary you set or need to set in your life. It is important that you understand the boundaries, misconceptions and how to solve the conflicts.

What are the right boundaries?

In life, many people may construe the term 'boundary' to be a selfish and demeaning aspect of a human social life. It is, therefore, important to understand the right boundaries, when and where to have them and for what purposes. Everyone needs to outline the right boundaries in life.

Misconceptions around boundaries

Life boundaries have been founded on misunderstandings over the years. Many people mistake these life practices to be

- ✓ an excuse for not helping other people or having an excuse to do what one wants

- ✓ limits meant for other people

- ✓ punishments for misbehavior

- ✓ boundaries are seen as walls to avoid relating with others

- ✓ as a means to control or change your children, friends, spouse or workmates

✓ using irrational means to control other people

More often than not, people who have a misunderstanding on the use of boundaries in life are known to subscribe to the expression *'setting boundaries'* is a show of selfishness and lack of submission. This is not true about boundaries. Most people have been fed with mischievous information regarding boundaries to the point of developing fear. Get all you need to know to begin setting the right boundaries in life.

Keen aspects

Never mind- there is more to setting boundaries than mere creation of limitation to others. The whole idea is about learning and practicing self-control in life. A boundary is more of a property line- it clearly earmarks the beginning and end of anything. Like in the physical world where the term could mean indicating ownership and the extent of one's responsibility, boundaries in the emotional, social and mental setting remain as important though intangible. These are property lines that define a person- who one is or is not.

Central to the setting life boundaries is the need to maintain healthy boundaries that are core to your personality. To begin, the following 3 steps could come in handy:

i.   *Check your personal engine light* – the human life is a product of the decisions taken upon certain indications. Every situation in life comes with a warning. You need to come up with a personal 'boundary' system to allow rational actions. These are indications that will help your system in controlling the entire body.

In this case, you can now tell when your boundaries are breached. Well-guarded boundaries will allow you to deal with all sorts of unwanted stuff. The initial step in establishing life boundaries is to understand the personal engine lights.

ii.   *Be ready to maintain and defend your boundaries –* always get the right tools to deal with the stormy moments of your life. The boundaries you have set must be held central to one's connection. With a firm root system, you can always defend from being blown. It allows for focus and connection with one's intuition and heart. Some of the known ways of grounding unto the set boundaries include:

- Meditation

- Affirmation

- Chanting your affirmations

- Use some phrases and relevant symbols for easy remembrance

iii.   *Be open to expression of feelings –* this allows clear understanding of your feelings between you and your children, your wife, friends or workmates. It is important that you take note of any situations that may aggravate them. However, it is not advisable to use any form of gifts to convince your friends or family, especially when you are guilty.

Boundaries and Responsibility

Worth noting is the fact that all the boundaries and limits you set out will come with some fair share of responsibilities. All that is within your boundaries is under your control. Make sure you can handle the situation to avert taking in unwanted stuff.

Everyone needs some form of help from either family, spouses, friends or workmates. To manage the tough times that may arise, it is advisable that you seek help and agree to such help when needed. Responsibility and boundaries implies that one can control what comes in and what goes out. As the person setting out the life boundaries, you need to be aware of the various people being affected by the boundaries. Your kids or spouse, workmates or friends will always look up to you for some advice on the limits.

At home, as the head of the family you need to clearly set the time for everything. Make sure you take responsibility of any ideals you need the family to subscribe. Your children will always seek further clarification on these ideals and you need to make them understood. At the workplace, leadership skills are exemplary when setting boundaries. This helps one to show some importance for the boundaries set out. Friends must relate positively based on the ideals they have spelt to follow as a group. This is what defines you as a person- your boundaries.

Chapter 10
Fundamentals of Life Boundaries

The need to come with boundaries is always central to our human nature. 'If you don't stand for something, you can fall for anything'. This is a phrase that often helps to know why we do things the way we do them. Boundaries are very important in guiding our social life. The benefits may vary from one social setting to another as highlighted below:

Having Marriage Boundaries

Marriage relationships are known to demand clear and strict boundaries. This is the closest of all human relationships. A stable and developing marriage is banked on freedom, love, protection and responsibility.

Put together, the above cornerstones of marriage create a stable relationship. It has been established that over time, with growth in love, spouses tend to become freer with each other. They turn away from vices like sinful patterns, self-centeredness, self-limitations and past wounds. This results into some sense of responsibility and self-control. The pillars of the relationship are known to develop each other over and over again.

Lack of freedom creates some sort of slavery causing rebellion. On the other hand, a responsibility vacuum ends in bondage and selfishness. This can only get better if there are boundaries. Blaming the other person is a common phenomenon in a relationship that has no boundaries. There is always need to own up to our mistakes instead of blaming on anyone else. Temporarily, our minds may get convinced that this has solved the problem but in the actual sense it has not.

Limits in a marriage helps to outline what every spouse is responsible for in the relationship. This helps to eliminate unnecessary blames and dangling of one's tasks. Relationships are ever faced by tides. The best way is to come up with a way that allows for equal participation in solving the situation. There is always a misconception that spouses setting out some limitations could endanger the relationship. This is a fear we need to deal with to ensure our marriage relationships grow deeper. The boundaries can only cause temporary flux; one that is very normal in relationships, but the benefits out rightly supersedes the lack of setting some.

Marriage is a social relationship that requires a deep sense of protection. Spouses must feel their relationship is protected by the other spouse. In a healthy marriage relationship, boundaries are set to help in safeguarding the good while protecting it from the evil. Unfortunately, some marriages have the 'silent sufferer'. This is where an abusive situation is known to trigger some unwarranted boundaries that eventually kill off the intensity of the relationship. To save the marriage, it is important that you stand by your boundaries and never let your spouse to abuse you. These are the firm limitations that will protect your relationship for the unthinkable. While this might be construed to be a sign for a divorce, this is not even an option. Come out and defend your marriage ideals to ensure continued happiness.

Within the boundaries

Every marriage intends to craft boundaries that are best for the development of their relationships. However, this could be a moving target unless spouses understand their responsibilities and take ownership of their tasks. This can only be possible if one identifies what is within the boundaries. These are the aspects of this relationship that spouses must protect and control. These include:

- **Attitudes and beliefs**- on one hand, beliefs are the issues one accepts to be the truth while on the other hand, attitude is one's perception of life, relations and other people among other aspects. These are aspects everyone develops at a tender age and hardly questions them at his or her old age. This could make us misunderstand what one should take responsibility for in life. The various convictions and attitudes are usually within our boundaries and we need to control them.

- **Feelings**- this is an inevitable phenomenon in the human nature. Feelings could cause us to do the unexpected in life. However, they should never be considered negative since they could motivate us into doing some great things. Anger, hurt or depressions are some of the negative feelings that must be addressed to avoid messing up. We must develop a culture of taking responsibility of our feelings. This way, we can control and protect them.

- **Behaviors**- in a marriage relationship, it is expected of every partner to give and receive love. Irresponsibility comes with a huge cost such as poverty, failure and other problems. We need to exercise self-control and stick to some ideals- the limits. The best way to control our behavior is taking full responsibility of it. This helps to avoid the notion that we act in a certain way due to bad luck or hate from nemesis.

- **Values**- anyone has what he or she loves and how important it is. This is controlled by our values. This often sets out our priorities such as the need to seek approval from others; valuing wealth, power or posh lifestyles. Lack of responsibility and discipline for our values may cause us to fight for so many things only to admire more once we get them. Married couples must understand the due value of their values, control them and take responsibility of their desires and values.

- **Choices**- the choices we make as human beings are always within our control. It is our responsibility to make them and bear any consequences. Distancing yourself from an awful choice will never solve any mess. We always shirk it off by blaming it on someone else or coming up with circumstances.

- **Limits**- in marriages and life in general, limits are mistaken to be meant for others. This is not true- you cannot make someone else acting 'rightly'. The best thing we can do is to come up with limits on the exposure to others. One could easily fall for his or her desires, feelings, or impulsive reactions. This underscores the need to have strict and rational limits to curb the above problems. It is upon every relationship partner to set up ways of observing self-control that is void of repression.

- Other aspects that are under our relationship boundaries include talents, thoughts, consequences, emotional and physical distance, and other people among others. We can always contain these for a better relationship with spouses.

A marriage is a union between two complete individuals. There is need for high level of maturity to avoid imbalance in the relationship. Maturity is not a matter of being a perfect person. Rather, as an adult, you can relate well with others and take action as deemed by the current situation. This is the ability to:

- overcome selfishness

- provide

- have self-confidence

- be responsible

- handle failures and problems in life

- be self-sufficient and independent

- understand and listen to others

- build and sustain a friendship

Having Boundaries at Work

There is need to positively relate at work: juniors and their seniors or juniors versus their fellow juniors as well as seniors amongst other seniors. It takes respect beyond fear or pressure to have a lively office. There are operational practices and guidelines to help in smooth running of the office. These could be ineffective if there are boundaries at work. The extent of personal interventions at the workplace should be guided by these limits.

Boundaries at work should begin with personal limits. As an individual, it is important that you come up with boundaries that you identify with at work. This grows into an office setting where everyone agrees on the boundaries. There are common problems that could be taken care of once you have stable working boundaries. They include:

- ✓ Ego- many people fail to understand their extent of intervention. Your ego could be a deterrent while working with others in an office. Boundaries at work will help to control this vice.

- ✓ Laxity at work- without boundaries, some people may tend to grow very lazy. It is important that you subscribe to some ideals as an office. These are necessary in controlling what one does in the office. This way, everyone is responsible and self-sufficient.

- ✓ Self-centeredness at work- once you have established your boundaries on how to relate with your workmates, it is easy embracing each other. This way, you can avoid making every situation all about you. You will always take time to listen and understand others.

Creating limits at work promotes better working relations and productivity. Boundaries at work will spur the following:

- Pro-activity- no one waits for a directive. With boundaries, everyone knows their responsibilities. This helps every workmate to act on their discretion to ensure a proactive mode of operation in the office.

- Induces self-confidence in the office- once you understand the relationship at work, it is easy working with each other. This is a sense of independence and confidence boost. With confidence, productivity is guaranteed in the office.

- Stronger ties at work- boundaries create a sense of ownership and responsibility at work. Everyone knows when to begin or stop a task. This way, you can correctly deal with each other in the office. Limits will not cause furor in the office but create stronger working ties amongst workmates.

Creating Boundaries with Friends

This is the second most influential social circle in life- friends. Everyone needs to have one. These are the people you share so much in life. The extent of their influence could be harmful or quite helpful depending on how you approach the relationship.

This guide highlights on the need to have clear boundaries with your friends to ensure a healthy relationship. It is true that most of our decisions are either misguided or advised by the people we share so much in common. Our friends could be right or wrong depending on what advices we share. The limits of our relationship should always remain clear to avert wasting each other's ideas and time.

There are many benefits associated with having boundaries with friends. These may include:

✓ Better understanding- when you learn each other's likes and dislikes, it is easy to live in harmony. Friends with boundaries always take time to listen and understand one another.

✓ Sense of protection- everyone has that friend he or she can trust with their secrets and life issues. This person often offers you an alternative when it seems impossible. When you have boundaries, your friends will always be there for you- protect you.

- ✓ Development in responsibility- friends with boundaries help to induce some sense of responsibility. Each of your friends has a role to play. A friend will make you realize your tasks and how to own up to your problems.

- ✓ Self-confidence and freedom- with boundaries, every friend feels free to address an issue without infringing on others. The boundaries you have set out will always help in controlling the relationship. This creates a high level of confidence in oneself thus better understanding and freedom amongst friends.

Lack of boundaries with friends may attract huge costs such as:

- Blinded friendship- a blind friendship is one without any positive vision. This is a group that will never come out to defend the talents or values of others. These are friends who spend more time without understanding each other's situations. Lack of boundaries may mean allowing anything from any of your friends thus hindering your personal progress.

- Lack of responsibility- having friends without limits means no one takes up any situation and own it up. This is a serious situation and friends can end up in a single stage of their lives. Friends must develop each other's sense of responsibility.

- Break ups- friends stand a huge risk of parting prematurely if there are no boundaries. With limits, everyone understands the vision of individuals and the group at large. This could be impossible in absence of boundaries. Life with friends is short-lived without limits.

Boundaries with Children and Family

A good family is banked on some values. These are ideals you subscribe to as a family. Children do not yelling and punishments to do the right thing- they need love and attention from their parents. In most cases, parents spend more energy to quarrel their kids while they take little time to listen to their situations.

To have a happy family, you need to set the right boundaries for your family. Take time to listen to them and say no to the unnecessary. This way, you will learn to accept to their essential quests. This is the first step towards implementing your set out boundaries- knowing your children.

Children will not respect you just because you are their parents. It takes virtue and good parenting for children to understanding why they should respect you. Once you have the right limits for your children, it is time to make sure they understand and adhere. This is the tricky part and most important of all. You need to listen and share with every kid at their personal level. Sometime during the night out or a snuggle-time before bed could be a good time to share with your kids. This allows you to evaluate their view on the family boundaries and their personal needs.

Work on the physical boundaries

The emotional boundaries with your children are highly impacted by the way kids internalize the physical boundaries. You need to make sure you have created stable physical boundaries. Such limits include movie time, time to bed, bathroom time and time to play and table time among others. Your children must have a stable ground of such practices before they can develop their understanding on the intangible values. For instance, if you just walk into your kids' bedroom without knocking, this could develop negatively and often they will bump on to your room in a similar manner. Punishments should be guided to avoid negative impacts as well.

Children too need respect. For example, playing and wrestling with your kids is physical bonding tool. However, they need to come out with an understanding that their physical requests are worthwhile. If a kid says stop, you need to do so immediately. This way, they are likely to respect other people's physical boundaries as they grow older.

Healthy life boundaries with our children help to teach children that they are a product of their own personality. This way, they will respect you as a parent and understand that no one else can define them. This creates a sense of freedom and independence.

Why boundaries

Children can only grow to understand and practice family boundaries. These are values they will always try to uphold and protect throughout their generations. Setting limits on the type of dresses they wear, friends they have, when to do anything at home or elsewhere will be a key guide to their lifestyle. Boundaries help to create understanding at home, harmony and freedom. Other benefits include:

- ✓ Better development- with limits, parents can develop their kids. This shapes them as they grow old. Boundaries will tune their lifestyle in a desired manner.

- ✓ Instills discipline and a sense of responsibility- a family that subscribes to some ideals will always own up to their issues in life. Children with boundaries grow to understand what they should do at certain times. This is a great sense of self-discipline and responsibility.

✓ Protection- it is the best feeling in a family when children feel protected by their parents. In return, parents who share some life boundaries with their children develop a feeling of protection as well. This way, the family values and ideals are safeguarded even for generations.

✓ It is easy solving conflicts in the family- arbitrating conflicts at home becomes easier if you have set out boundaries. Everyone understands their position in the family thus easier to deal with misunderstandings.

Chapter 11
Boundary Conflict Resolution

Boundaries in life are not always welcomed. Due to either lack of clarity or misconstrued sense of internalization of the boundaries, you might have to deal with resistance and irresponsibility among other conflicts. Your spouse, children, friends or workmates could have one problem or another with your boundaries.

To resolve on the conflicts that have arisen from the set boundaries, it is important that you do the following:

- Develop patience and self-control. This helps to control your feelings towards a rebellious spouse or friend. Take your time to understand the cause of their resistance before acting on it.

- Appreciate your family, friends and workmates for who they are. Do not jump into conclusions but always make sure you listen and reason out together.

- Be open to criticism and correction. While you might have the boundaries set, allow for dialogue and correction in case a friend, spouse or child feels to have a different opinion.

- Be sympathetic and accommodating. The boundaries could come at a time when your friends or family are facing tricky situations. Always find space to share their problems that could be hindering them from observing your boundaries. Show empathy to their needs, desires and hurts.

There are various aspects life boundaries that we need to change so as to have a smooth relationship with our children, spouses, workmates or friends. These are:

o Allowing others to say no to what they feel is not worthy

o Having a heart to forgive others' faults

o Find respect for others' freedom

o Be honest to others without feeling afraid

o Be compassionate with your friends, family or workmates on their negative feelings and weaknesses

o Do not become so controlling over anyone or anything

o Be ready to apologize and accept confrontation when you fault others

Key elements that you need to consider when resolving boundary conflicts are:

✓ *Observation*- alwaysbe on the lookout for any rebellion. Always take time to check for any weaknesses in your spouse, friends, workmates and children.

✓ *Confrontation*- upon realization of a fault, you should confront the person without fear. This way, you will resolve the issue easily. Additionally, you could be on the wrong. Admit to you mistakes and allow other to conflict you on the same.

✓ *Ownership*- develop a sense of ownership. Your children, friends or workmates should learn to own up to their mistakes and take full responsibility. Avoid blaming others for your mistakes or creating circumstantial reasons.

✓ *Repentance*- ask for forgiveness when on the wrong and accept apologies from others when they fault you.

✓ *Communication*- for better understanding, always discuss on issues at hand. Communication allows for effective resolutions in case of any boundary conflicts.

✓ *Re-evaluation*- once there is a boundary in place, make sure you sit back and examine its effectiveness. Allow others to understand the limits and check on the importance once more.

Causes of Boundary Resistance

Once the boundaries have been set, maintaining and protecting them could be tricky. It is even difficult dealing with resistance and resolving the conflicts that arise. This demands some self-discipline and understanding. Common causes of such resistances are:

- Empathic failure

- Irresponsibility

- Feeling pressed when subjected to limits

- Living in the imperfection denial

- Unnecessary desire to be in control and power

- Quest for a retaliation

- Transference

Empathic failure

Empathic failure has become a normal characteristic feature in most relationships; they are often regarded as small failures to fulfill certain obligations. It can be referred to as involuntarily recognizing boundaries set by others , hence Empathic failure are pardonable to certain extent, however, when such failures become rampant, the other partner whose boundary is being invaded may take serious actions against the culprit. Through empathic failures one can learn to identify boundaries set by others, hence Empathic failures should not be seen as negative but a constructive problem that will help an individual become more aware of such boundaries after facing the consequences of his actions.

Irresponsibility

Irresponsibility is a deliberate act, and unlike Empathic failure, Irresponsibility are viewed as more grievous and the consequences set against irresponsible behaviors are tougher than those set against Empathic failure. When a partner is not committed to recognizing the boundaries set by the other, there will always be a friction of interest. Irresponsibility is the most prominent cause of boundary resistance and it is often the most difficult factor to handle in any relationship.

Feeling pressed when subjected to limits

Most people who break boundary limits do so because they feel they have been subjected to boundary limits. Many people think that setting boundaries in relationships shows that their spouses are secretive. A successful marriage should be based on open-mindedness, and the setting of boundaries to some spouses means their spouses cannot be trusted. A spouse has a reason for setting boundaries, and the other person does not have to see him or her as being secretive. When a spouse feels he is being subjected to restrictions, he is bound to react and such reactions may either make or mare the relationship at the long run.

Living in the imperfection denial

One of the main reasons why boundaries are resisted is that some spouses are denying the fact that they are imperfect. When a spouse is denying her imperfection, she will try to shield her shame by creating boundaries, so that the other partner does not get to remind her of that imperfection. When you are perfect, you don't have to worry about anything, and your boundaries are usually easier to protect, however, when you have something to hide, your boundaries may become unrealistic and that could hurt the other partner the more.

Unnecessary desire to be in control and power

Many men are guilty of this issue- they want to stay in control and power and ensure that their partners don't know what they do in secret. When an individual wants to remain in power always, he tries as much as possible to impose numerous boundaries that make it difficult for anyone to track him down, however such habits will often lead to confrontational arguments with spouses who believe they are being subjected to unreasonable boundaries. The partner who often desire to be in control and power is often seen as an aggressor, and it is difficult for the other partner not to violate his boundaries.

Quest for a retaliation- Most women who set unnecessary boundaries often do so as a quest for retaliation against previous actions taken by their spouses. Quest for retaliation is an act that can bring discourse between couples and may even end a relationship if not properly handled. A woman may seek retaliation against a cheating husband for instance and banish him from sharing a bed with her for several weeks or months. Many boundaries set as a result of quest for retaliation often end up as destructive correctional methods.

Transference

When a partner had been cheated upon in the past, he or she may transfer the anger generated from such experience to a new partner, and he or she does this by setting out some boundaries. In most cases, a woman may set transference boundaries in order to avoid coming in contact with situations that remind her of the past. Transference could be response to trauma, and until the wounds of such trauma heels, an individual will continue to set boundaries.

Resolving boundary conflicts in marriage

In several cases a resistant spouse may not see the hidden benefits of relational boundaries within the marriage. Most men are the ones who always end up bursting all the boundaries in their marriages, and their wives don't take such offences lightly always. Spouses who try to control their partners know that change is always painful and they hear that they are inflicting hurtful feelings on the people they love but they keep doing such things because they have little or no control over their own feelings .Making changes in marriage boundaries may involve several things including the following;

- Accepting and allowing your spouse to say No to you when you cross the boundaries,

- Admitting to the fact that you have been trying to exercise excessive control over your spouse

- Submitting yourself to the process of learning self-control especially on how to stay within the boundaries,

- Respecting your partner's freedom,

- Learning the ability of restraining yourself from attacking or withdrawing from your spouse or even make her feel guilty during conflicts,

- Having the awareness of your helpless state to control anyone, and

- Learning to ask your partner for her comments or feedbacks especially when you cross her boundaries.

The tasks mentioned above are not normally pleasant when resolving boundary conflicts in marriage, it is understandable, just like it hurts sometimes to accept that there are boundaries in marriages. It is also important to understand that conflict resolution in marriage is painful but it is a pain that will end up on a positive note.

One of the problems couples face with the issue of boundaries in marriage is that the boundary-loving spouse cannot tolerate the boundary-resistant partner, the boundary-loving spouse does not grasp the idea that the boundary resistant partner does not feel the same as she does, however, understanding the other partner's viewpoints will help you handle issues the right way and more serious complications can be avoided. Here are some of the conclusions experts have made about individuals boundaries issues in marriages;

- Partners who do not respect the boundaries set by others do possess a basic attitude towards life in general; "I should be able to do whatever I want, whenever I want to". Some partner often wants ultimate freedom as their privilege or right. While parents notice this trait in their kids, they believe such kids will outgrow such issues and learn to respect people's boundaries in the future.

- Some spouses may break boundary rules, but they remain wonderful and loving in character. He may be breaking your boundaries occasionally but he genuinely and deeply cares about your progress, health and every other thing, and couples that find themselves in this situation may live comfortably until issues of boundaries arise and then the good feelings suddenly disappear, giving way to feelings of guilt, anger or even acting out of place.

- The boundary resistant spouse react in his own way because he feels that any limit in a relationship is unfair an unreasonable. A boundary-resistant partner will become so mean at his partner for pushing him out of some particular restricted areas of her life. Her simple requests to respect her privacy may suddenly mean hate or unrighteousness to him. For the men, it is unreasonable to start feeling immature and angry simply because your partner has set limits or boundaries.

Accepting and allowing your spouse to say No to you when you cross the boundaries

Accepting and allowing your spouse to say No when you cross the boundaries, is the simplest way of handling boundary issues in marriages. When you accept a simple No for an answer, you will learn to cope and handle pressures from breaking her rules. Accepting your spouse' No can be painful, it may force you to feel restricted or rejected in certain ways, whereas the reverse is a case. Women generally set boundaries and they appreciate when their men accept and honor such boundaries. When you learn to adjust to her boundaries, you will naturally find it easier to stay out of trouble.

Submitting yourself to the process of learning self-control especially on how to stay within the boundaries

If you find yourself always breaking the boundaries set by your spouse, then its time you submit yourself to the process of self-control. Exercising self-control can help you adjust your own lifestyles to ensure that you don't get caught up in situations that will make you cross the boundaries. There are several ways of submitting yourself to the process of learning self-control, first of all you need to understand the periods of time when you normally break into her boundaries, secondly, you need to identify alternative paths or actions you can take that will ensure that you do not break the boundaries again. For instance, if your spouse doesn't want the bedroom light on while she is sleeping but you still need to work late into the night, then you have to find an alternative place within your home to complete your tasks.

Respecting your partner's freedom

Respecting your partner's freedom is one of the easiest ways to avoid boundary disputes in marriage. Just because you are suspecting your partner of infidelity, does not mean you must invade her privacies always. Each and every woman deserves some privacies. As long as your partner is respecting your freedom, you must also respect her freedom, otherwise, there will always be conflicts. When you respect your partner's freedom, she will extend the same gesture towards you.

Learning the ability of restraining yourself from attacking or withdrawing from your spouse or even make her feel guilty during conflicts,

There are high possibilities that you will occasionally break the boundary rules, even if you apply extra cautions not to. In this case, you need to learn the act of restraining yourself from getting into confrontational arguments with your spouse. When you break the boundaries, you should learn to apologize immediately instead of being confrontational even after you have been caught. You don't have to enforce your right to know everything your spouse is doing, she would have communicated the boundaries to you before you got married to her, hence you must take responsibilities for breaking the rules. When you make her feel guilty during conflicts, she will become upset and even create new boundaries and that is what you should avoid at all cost.

Having the awareness of your helpless state to control anyone

One of the main reasons why boundary disputes arise in marriages is that the man always wants to be the main dominating force. He wants to control every aspect of the relationship, including financial decisions, and the woman may feel she is being cheated. Men who always seek the opinions of their partners in marriage before making any decision normally have little or no issues with boundaries. Being aware of your helpless state to control anyone should be seen as a psychological or emotional problem and the earlier you seek help, the earlier you can avoid confrontational situations as regards marital boundaries.

Learning to ask your partner for her comments or feedbacks especially when you cross her boundaries

Sometimes, you may not understand when you have crossed the boundaries in your relationship, and your partner will expect that you ask her or apologize even if you are not aware. Your partner's feedback should help when you find yourself in this situation. Most women exhibit irrational behavior – for instance, they keep quiet when they are hurt, and will refuse to tell you when they are unhappy with you. If your partner is not willing to communicate with you when you cross the boundaries, then you must be ready to figure it out by yourself and this could be painstaking.

Most of the tasks highlighted above can be extremely difficult for men but they will eventually pay off and help you stay safe from crossing the boundaries. It is now understandable that any spouse will definitely experience boundary exploitation or intrusion, and accepting boundaries will be hurtful especially for the men, it is quite important that some of the pains associated with learning to live with boundaries are growth-producing.

Establishing consequences for your spouse' transgression against your boundaries

As a woman, you may have to establish some consequences for your spouse especially if he continues to dis-respect the boundaries and doesn't want to change. These actions will make him feel discomfort for his deliberate actions. The consequences you set up must possess the following characteristics;

- o Must be realistic, and not designed to control or change your spouse – Creating boundaries and consequences for breaking through boundaries should not be about fixing a spouse and trying to make them be better off, rather they must be done to allow appropriate cause to take place and ensure that your spouse feel the pain of an irresponsible behavior.

- o Must not be deliberate or impulsively conceived out of anger- When setting the penalties for your partner who is pushing beyond the boundaries, you must not do so out of anger, otherwise the situation may become even more complex. Make sure you think through, and decide on the most appropriate punishment that will be corrective in nature, rather than being destructive in nature. You need to consider the fact that such penalties must not be aimed at getting even, it should done to protect yourself against the negative affects you may face when your boundaries were violated.

- o Must be reality-based as possible- You definitely want your spouse to come back to reality, and people are always wary of staying around people who play tantrums , hence the consequences you set must be realistic enough not to make him turn worse.

76

o Must be appropriately severe in effect- Consequences against boundary violation in marriage must be proportionately severe (must not be too harsh nor too lenient). In order to set the best consequences, you need to evaluate how destructive or severe the boundary violation is. For instance, if your spouse refuses to clean dishes when he needs to, then you should allow him to cook his meals to get the idea of the consequences of his actions. A spouse who is having extra marital affair will require more serious punishment, but it must not be too severe to cause destructive actions.

o Must be enforceable under any circumstances – You need to ensure that the consequences you set can be done and be controlled. You need to be sure of your resources and the ability to set limit at which your boundaries may be broken. Do not set punishments that are beyond your own control, otherwise, the situation may get out of control.

o Must preserve the freedom of your spouse- You don't just set consequences by words of mouth, and remember that consequences are not set up to control your spouse, rather they are correctional measures or reactions to the negative choices he is making. You need to allow your spouse make his choices while you set your own reactions.

o Must be immediate as possible- The consequences you set against a spouse who violate the boundaries must be quick. Just as the kids require constant and quick response to their decisions, older adults like spouses also require instant correctional reactions when they cross the boundaries. Your spouse needs to establish a connection between his actions and the reactions he will get, this will help him refrain from crossing the boundaries and consider the consequences of his actions before acting.

o   Must recognize and respect his roles as a partner or spouse- You must not set consequences for boundary rules by saying " You must" or " I will make sure you do...", rather, such consequences must recognize his roles, hence it must not be aimed at humiliating him. You must not create punitive consequences or make fun of him through some sarcastic remarks.

o   Must be designed for modification- The consequences set must be able to undergo periodic modification, as your spouse returns to reality and abide by the rules of boundaries set by you. As your spouse repents from his actions, you must reduce the severity of the consequences of his actions. You need to be however sure that his changes are genuine, and do not rely on words such as "I'm sorry", but his actions must clearly shows that he has changed. You may also have to increase the severity of some consequences if you believe your spouse is not changing for the better.

There will always be some difficult realities when setting boundaries in marriage, especially when dealing with an un-corporative spouse. When your spouse does not support limits being set, then you need to make it a gradual process starting with a thorough explanation of the reasons why you are setting the boundaries but remember that , it is not advisable to threaten your spouse because you want to set boundaries.

Resolving boundary disputes with professional colleagues

Resolving boundary disputes at work can be as difficult as marriage boundary resolution, and the reason being that conflicts are inevitable at an organization where different people have different expectations. Boundary conflicts at work can be avoided in so many ways, whether through avoidance of arguments, or through a tougher option of litigation, it all depends on how an individual is able to manage such disputes. Some companies normally provide full time mediators in organizations, and these people investigate and ensure that all disputes are carefully examined before passing judgments or resolving the disputes. Here are some options you must consider for settling boundary disputes before they become full-blown conflicts;

- Stay calm and don't be unruffled,

- Listen and understand the other party

- Emphasize more on the positive,

- Tactfully state your case,

- Attack the issue and not the person,

- Stay away from the blame game,

- Focus more on the future and not the past,

- Throw the right kind of questions,

- Tactically, pick your battles, and

- Be creative about the conflict resolution.

Stay calm and don't be unruffled- Nothing else can give you more advantage over the other person while resolving boundary disputes than staying calm and unruffled under all circumstances. Escalation is often the main factor that can trigger conflicts, and anger is the main issue that triggers the escalation of conflicts in boundary disputes. As you get angry, it becomes difficult for you to listen, before you argue back. When you stay calm you will be able to point out the flaws in the other person's arguments, and if you picture it right now, you will notice that all boundary disputes will eventually become resolved after all points of arguments have been considered.

The work environment is becoming increasingly difficult to manage even with the increasing number of PDAs, emails and cellphones- many clients still can't get enough support and such working conditions will create even more stress. When conflicts arise at work, the first thing you should be thinking of is; what can I contribute to end this boundary conflicts? It is very important to check your faults and remain calm in order to avoid embarrassing yourself when you finally discover that you are at fault.

Listen and understand the other party- Paying careful attention is the most important step towards boundary resolution at work place. You can learn the act of listening an understanding the other person by picturing a recent dispute you were involved. Take for instance, yesterday morning, while leaving the house, you were involved with a boundary confrontation with a family member, client or colleague at work. Try as much as possible to replay your experience, and as you do this, you must ask yourself; how much listening actually took place during the argument? The probability that any listening took place during the argument will be extremely low, because each person wants to prove his point. The best possible way of resolving a boundary dispute is to stop and listen for a while, and when you listen to what other person has got to say, you can point out the errors or omissions he is committing and such errors could win the argument in your favor at the end.

Other people will always surprise you with reasons and when you listen more, you will easily discover that people's underlying interests are the reason why they create boundary disputes, they will keep arguing until they drop a point where you can prove them wrong- but how will you discover this when you are busy arguing with them while they were talking. People will usually start out by downgrading the other person's points of view, they will also personalize issue and want their own intentions override others and they end up speaking with anger.

Psychologists have made it clear that anger is usually the secondary emotion that used as a defense mechanism that can be used in covering up fear and hurt. When someone is angry, it often occurs that there is something he is afraid of, and in order to diffuse the other person's anger, you need to learn to listen to them. You will notice that most people who start their arguments on an angry note tend to slow down when they see that you are not arguing with them. Actively listening during a boundary resolution at work will signal some verbal signs to people that you understand what they are saying. Simple gestures such as nodding, or saying "okay" will reassure the other person that you are on their sides and ready to welcome their points.

When you are attending to clients on phone, at work, giving a dead silence to a client means you are not listening to their complaints, and they may fear the worst and possibly shut down the conversation, but when you occasionally give your consents by saying "Okay" intermittently, they know you are following them and will eventually pause and let you speak- this is when you are re-establish your boundaries and let them know when they are crossing the boundaries.

You cannot achieve a conflict resolution until the experiences of each participant has been fully heard, especially as regards their perspectives on the subject of matter. When you set boundaries, and there seems to be a clash of interest, the other person may think that you don't care about them. You should act as a good customer representative of your company, even if you don't work in that professional capacity, but the ability to let people finish their complaints before voicing your opinion will help you resolve boundary disputes faster and easier. Get all the "broken pieces" on a table and then glue them together- this is how you resolve conflicts.

In most confrontational arguments about boundary disputes, the commonest questions you will hear others ask are; can I ask you a question? What is so important to you? Or why are you so selfish? When you hear these questions then you should consider keeping quiet for a while and let the person talking express his or her frustration or anger before explaining your point. If you are at fault, the first thing you should do when it is your time to talk is to first apologize, and take full responsibility for your actions, however, let them realize that you have boundaries and they must respect such.

Emphasize more on the positive- When you emphasize or accentuate on the positive, you can easily discover some common points of agreements between you and the other person involved in the conflict resolution. Even if you do not end up on an agreeable terms, then you can simply tell the other person that he or she must give you some time to work things out and this will normalize things eventually.

Normalizing the situation by focusing on the positive side of things can calm people immediately.

Tactfully state your case

Learning to state your case tactfully is one of the best possible ways of resolving boundary conflicts successfully. The key to resolving issues is to let people understand things from your own perspective without making them become more defensive. You can eventually disarm people from their frustration and anger by tending a tactfully prepared case, and you can be tactful with your case by stating what is yours, but you must apologize for your wrongdoing first. Try as much as possible to avoid stating issues of differences, however you must leave some little benefits of doubt. You don't have to insist on certain issues and try to acknowledge some room of doubt- this will make the other person feel at ease and ready to shift his position in your favor.

Try as much as possible to state your position along with your interest or boundaries, and what this means is that; instead of not acknowledging that nothing is wrong, it is better you offer a position that will be helpful such as providing a perspective that they will also benefit by respecting your boundaries. You need to remember that your position is the bottom line of your argument, while your interests or boundaries are the main reasons behind such arguments. If your boundary or interest will take something away from others, you should offer something back in compensation or simply try and respect their own interests or boundaries too. Tactfully stating your case is the best possible way of dis-arming the other person, and it will simply take the fight away from the argument.

Attack the issue and not the person- Most people lose out in boundary disputes because they attack the other person instead of attacking the main issue. When you de-personalize your points, your views can be easily heard and accepted. You should focus on saying things like "we will have to deal with this issue together" rather than saying "You have to deal with the issue". You don't have to drive home your point by personalizing and even cursing people just because they break through your boundaries. Maintaining an ideal concentration while arguing with people will help you avoid personalizing the issue and that will help avoid conflicts.

Stay away from the blame game

Try as much as possible to avoid assigning blames when trying to resolve boundary disputes at work. If you have to assign any blame then you have to assign it to yourself. When you accuse people of violating your boundaries, you may end up messing things up, and if the goal is to fix a problem, it doesn't worth it spending too much time on the blame game. The blame game is a diversion and will end up costing more on conflict resolution because you have to sort out and investigate the person at fault. The real trick on solving issues is to focus more attention on resolving issues instead of pointing accusing fingers. You need to focus on your individual strengths and see where both parties can compromise to bring an amicable resolution to the boundary issues.

Focus more on the future and not the past- The solutions to boundary issues start and end with present and future tenses and not the past. You don't have to spend much time on what went wrong and who did what wrongly but the real solution is to treat the situation with a problem-solving approach. Though the past can be analyzed in order to ensure that the problem does not repeat itself. The solution is what you should be interested in.

Learn to throw the right kind of questions- The best possible way of detecting that someone is violating your boundaries is through the asking of the right type of questions. When you ask the other person questions such as; what or why is that? Or what in your opinion do you think it should be? Then you will end up making him more defensive. Make sure you ask him the future and present tense questions because that is the only way you can resolve boundary conflicts and that is how you can find solutions to a problem.

Sometimes, some people ask short and direct questions and the other person will perceive they are interrogating them instead of trying to resolve issues. Some questions will help you get what you want to get from someone while other questions will permit you to tell them what they ought to know- you should aim at the latter, because you cannot communicate your boundaries to people without first telling them, and when you tell them where your boundaries, lie, they can't claim ignorance of not knowing.

Try as much as possible to give people a little information first by telling them why you are asking them such questions, then you will be able to make your intention clear at first and they wouldn't have to guess it. Asking the right question will help deliver your facts and will help you reach an amicable negotiation. Asking the right questions will also make the other person less defensive.

Another type of question that can help you get more information from a boundary conflict is the Open-ended type of question, they are also referred to as Opposite or directive questions and such questions will help invite the other person about what he thinks about the boundary dispute or what is important in the present situation- these include questions such as "Can you tell me what actually went wrong at the beginning?" or "It sounds as if this situation seemed too frustrating to you?" The answers or information you obtain from Open-ended questions like these can help you get more information that can help you resolve boundary disputes at work.

Tactically, pick your battles- When asking questions during boundary disputes, it is important to choose your points tactically. The natural instinct in man will want us to be right at all time, even to the extent of defending a point that may not really matter at the end. Tactically picking your battles during boundary conflict resolution will help you throw tactical questions such as "On a scale of 1 to 5, how important do you think this issue is to you?" If an issue is rated 2 by the other person and 4 to you, on a scale of 5, then there is no point arguing on the issue, however, if the issue is of equal importance to the two of you then you can continue resolving the issue.

Many people think the issue of boundary setting should be 50-50, however, there is no argument on boundary disputes that will put each party at equal rights- when issues are adjusted based on individual's perspectives, an argument is bound to favor someone than the other. In boundary resolution, you should either choose whether you are right or whether you want to be happy.

Be creative about the conflict resolution- Just because you set boundaries does not mean they are undisputable or non-negotiable. You can actually resolve boundary conflicts more easily by being creative and open-minded. You need to think outside the box occasionally with your boundaries and see where your interests are clashing with the interest of others and see where you can make compromises to ensure that an amicable resolution is brought in. Make sure your ideas are not fat-fetched. It is true that being creative with boundary resolutions may make such resolutions last longer, and at the end you can achieve a win-win solution.

You can be creative with boundary resolutions by carefully listening when asking open-ended questions, and then gathering information you can use later to bring success formula into your resolutions. You can propose creative solutions where the other person or persons may find it easier not to invade your privacy or cause boundary disputes in the future. Being creative with your resolution tactics may mean, you may have to shift your position as regards your boundaries- for instance, you can suggest alternative ways they can handle business issues without involving you, hence your interests will still be protected and they wouldn't step beyond the boundaries.

Be confident but don't be confrontational- Not getting confrontational when resolving boundary conflicts does not make you less confident, it simply shows you are matured enough to state your case without causing "bad blood" or friction between others and yourself. Don't be like many people who always shy away front confrontations, the reason being that you may never resolve boundary disputes that way and people will always violate your spaces or boundaries. Having confidence in yourself gives you the ability to convince others about how they can avoid violating your boundaries and avoid causing troubles.

Celebrate any boundary resolution victories you make- There is nothing wrong celebrating the victories achieved when you successfully resolve boundary disputes.

Celebrating with the other person after boundary resolution can build trust and friendship. You and the other person involved in the resolution deserve some pat in the back especially when you finally come into agreement. Nothing is more important than the survival of a relationship or friendship, hence you need to cultivate the habits of ensuring peace between yourself and others.

Chapter 12
Evaluating Boundary Success

After coming up with practical boundaries in life, there is need for fundamental adjustment to the way one thinks so as to uphold these boundaries. One is likely to get discouraged as the effects may take longer than expected. The process can be evaluated based on the following stages to check on the level of development and the next step to take in the process. The evaluation stages are:

- Anger- when your boundaries are infringed, the initial warning is being aggrieved. This, however, should be controllable and within your limits.

- Changes in personal preferences. As you begin the process, you begin getting attracted to the limitations. This creates a sense of control over the boundaries.

- Close connections to those with clear boundaries. You always find it easy identifying with those who have precise limits in their lives.

- Change in the value system. What you value begin changing as you establish a close connection with those who have clear boundaries.

- Safe environment to practice your boundaries

- Guilty feelings are a sign of growth. These are feelings associated to development in the sense of ownership.

- Trying your boundaries with difficult people.

- Disappearance of guilt feelings. As you develop, you get better ways of establishing the right boundaries and ways of safely solving any conflicts.

- Desire to involve others in boundaries

- Being sure of your decisions. When you have grown up the process of boundaries, it becomes easy to say NO instead of an uncertain acceptance.

- Setting goals that are visionary and value-driven.

Chapter 13
How to set up boundaries and achieve success

It is easier to identify stressed people in every spheres of life- they simply don't set boundaries, while some of them have boundaries but rarely monitor if someone is breaking through such boundaries. You need to learn how to set up personal boundaries in life, because such boundaries will help move towards success in every spheres of your life- whether marriage, financial, or business.

There are few steps you should take when setting up your personal boundaries, these are;

- Identifying what exactly personal boundaries are,

- Identify exactly what you want,

- Know where you are presently are,

- Create more value for your time,

- Identify good boundaries and realize that they can help you create better relationships,

Identify what exactly personal boundaries are- Simply put, a personal boundary is defined as a line that sets the limit. For instance, the lines marked on parking lots clearly indicate the boundaries where cars must park and any cars that violate such boundaries may be fined. You should consider the fact that without line boundaries in car park lots, fewer cars would probably fit into parking spaces because everyone will park haphazardly. In the same way boundaries are set at parking lots, so also personal boundaries can help you prevent frustrations, stress, resentment and failure in your everyday living.

Having personal boundaries will help improve your personal relationships, and helps you head toward the right direction while increasing your productivity at all fronts. Take for instance, when you are stranded on an Island, the first thing you do is to gather materials that can help you set a boundary and build a shelter for protection.

Know what you want – Knowing what you want is the most important building block in the setting up of boundaries. Once you know what personal boundaries are, you need to ponder and spend some time to identify what exactly you want in life. You can't set boundaries when you still don't understand what exactly you want. If you want to pursue a certain career then you need to identify key elements of that career that needs to have boundaries so that you can pursue the career successfully. Setting boundaries involve setting disciplinary steps that you must follow in other to accomplish your aims.

Know where you are presently are- knowing where you are presently can help you set the record straight on where you want to be. You need to identify the things bugging you now, likewise you need to identify key elements frustrating you, especially those obstacles causing frustration on your productivity- Productivity reduces when challenges become insurmountable and you become even more frustrated. You need to identify your strength and weaknesses, and then identify how you can use your strength to cover up your weaknesses so that you can improve on your productivity.

Create value for your time- You value your time when you stop doing what others bid on your, and doing what will enhance your own value. Time is as valuable as any other thing, and when you don't manage your time, it becomes more difficult to set boundaries and monitor them. When you value your time, you wouldn't allow constant interruptions to and this can reduce your self-worth and make you become less productive. You need to know what you are doing at a particular time and what you are achieving at that particular time, this will help ensure that your boundaries are effective.

Identify good boundaries and realize that they can help you create better relationships- You can only set your boundaries effectively by training others how to treat you, and when you communicate your limits to others, they will value and respect you , especially when they understand the consequences of violating your boundaries. People's interests don't have to clash with yours before boundary disputes are created.

Create boundary dispute resolutions- Now that you know how to start the process of creating boundaries, you should also create a way to resolve any boundary dispute that may arise when your interest clash with others. You don't have to become confrontational with people when they cross the boundaries because some people may be unaware of cross the boundaries. Boundary dispute resolutions will help put people back in their places and they can easily recognize when they are about to commit the same offence again.

Where to set your personal boundaries

There are several key areas of your life you must set boundaries around,however, there are specific areas you must consider first ahead of others, and these are;

- Time,

- Your responsibilities or tasks,

- The expectations from others,

- Your self-care, and

- Your space.

Your time – First and foremost, you need to set boundaries around your time if you want to become more productive and more successful. People, who don't set boundaries around their time, often end up doing the right things at the wrong time or the wrong things at the right time. When you set boundaries around your time, you will know when to work and when to engage in pleasure and your friends and family wouldn't violate such boundaries because they know where you are and what you are doing at a specific time.

If you think it's easy to get simple things such as a blog post done then you should wait till later in the day when unexpected things come up and get you distracted. You need to schedule appointments at realistic time and set boundaries or time limit for which you can break the rules of meeting appointments. You need to set up some self-constraints in order to ensure that you don't violate your own boundaries. You are not a super-human, but setting realistic boundaries around your time can help you become disciplined.

Your responsibilities or tasks – You need to set your boundaries around your tasks and remember that to a certain extent, your responsibilities will depend on others. Just as you expect others to fulfill their responsibilities, they likewise expect you to fulfill your obligations. When you don't have boundaries, you will naturally say yes to every work or duties thrown your way and that will only force you to pile up jobs you wouldn't be able to complete. Unexpected tasks may come up and you must incorporate them into your boundaries, if you don't want to suffer from exhaustion and stress later on.

Setting boundaries around your own tasks will help you complete them on time without having to seek the help of others. When you don't set boundaries around your responsibilities, you may end up becoming a burden to others.

The expectations from others – You need to set boundaries around what people expect from you. Just because you are the best in what you do does not mean you must turn yourself to a slave and trying to satisfy everyone. It is important that you communicate with your family, friends and colleagues about what you will do and what you will not do, and make plans with them especially on how you can help them at your spare time and how they can help you complete certain chores. If you have set new boundaries, you need to notify other, otherwise, you shouldn't blame them if they violate such boundaries.

Your self-care – If you do not set limit around yourself, you will gradually fall sick, overweight and malnourish. Having a sound health is the number one key to high productivity; hence you need to set limit to what you should accomplish on a daily basis and at a given time. You need to set boundaries in such a way that you can have sufficient time to rest, play, eat well and exercise when necessary. Setting boundaries around yourself will help you become disciplined and become more active or productive at the long run. Taking care of yourself may also means, taking care of several other things such as laundry, and other home chores- all these will require a substantial part of your time and failure to do them may interfere with your general quality of living and productivity.

You need to have a resolute mind and pay attention to your body when you work- when your body asks you to stop, you must not hesitate to stop working and take rest.

Your space- If you work in an organization, you may find it easier to set boundaries around your space, but when you work from home, it becomes more difficult to set boundaries around your space. You need to let everyone around you understand the limits or rules around your office supplies, and you need to let them know that constant interruptions and distractions can create some frustration and make you become less productive. You need to let your family, friends, and colleagues understand that violating your space may result in chaos, loss of office items or even breakages of some sensitive items, hence they need to respect your space.

Steps and Actions to take in creating personal boundaries

If you believe that you may need to set some boundaries in order to survive and become prosperous, you should do so by engaging in the following practical steps;

- o Start small – You need to evaluate each area of your life causing frustrations, and work at one particular area at a time. You will discover that setting boundaries in one key area of your life will motivate you to set up boundaries in every other areas. If not having enough time to attend to your extra office works is the issue, or if many co-workers like using your office supplies, you can start setting boundaries around such situations and ensure that not everyone has access to your office supplies- this will force co-workers respect your space and find their own supplies elsewhere. When you start small, you can gradually attend to other areas of your life that need boundaries.

o Take notes and write down what you expect from each areas of your life- You may have to spend a couple of intense and highly focused period of time to write down what you expect in each area of your life. For instance, if you want to stop other workers from using your office supplies excessively, you can simply write "My office supplies will be for my personal use from now". The more you obey this rule, the easier you find it easier to maintain your boundaries.

o Cut out the emotion and consider where you are right now! Sometimes, you may have to cut own your emotions when creating personal boundaries. If social media networking for instance are interrupting your abilities to stick with your rules, then you need to work on your emotions in such a way that you don't spend too much time on such distractions- If you have been spending 2 hours a day on social media, you should aim at spending less than an hour a day, in order to have time for more serious activities. Your emotions could be your number one challenge in sticking with your boundaries.

o Have a list of the practical boundaries you can set and whoever will be involved with such boundaries- for instance , you can set a social media boundary such as " I will not check my Twitter account between 1pm and 3pm", or OFFICE- My office supplies will be used only by me. These two boundaries are physical boundaries that involve you only, hence you have to stick with them.

o Try as much as possible to communicate your boundaries to those who will be involved. This procedure will be important when you explain the problems to them, because they can help you set the boundaries. You should expect feedbacks from such people, especially on boundaries that may create some conflicts against their own interests- in this case, you must be prepared to make some adjustments or compromise before finalizing the boundaries.

o Make use of all tools necessary to set and enforce your boundaries – There are so many tools you can use in setting out and enforcing your boundaries, while some are automated, others are manual. Automated tools you can use in enforcing your boundaries include; computer updates, signals, reminders, and apps, while manual tools include; written manuals, and diaries. Boundary crating apps can help you block certain websites such as Twitter and Facebook at certain hours of the day, some apps can also help you set limits where certain activities will automatically shut out when the limits are reached.

o Perform a periodic evaluation on your boundaries and make adjustments when necessary- Performing a periodic evaluation on your boundaries can help you identify the boundaries that are unrealistic and need modification very fast. Some boundaries may set you against the management rules at work; hence you need to modify such rules so that you wouldn't get into trouble with the law.

The Importance of re-setting your boundaries

Setting up some clear personal boundaries is the surest way of ensuring that personal relationships turn to mutually respectful and supportive one. The personal boundaries you set will definitely measure your self-esteem, and they help you set the limit and the type of acceptable behaviors you want around you. Setting personal limits will ensure that people do not take advantage of you. If you are not comfortable with the way people treat you, it is the time you start setting personal boundaries, or if the boundaries existed before, now is the time to reset them and such will show others that you deserved to be respected also.

If you find it difficult to reset your boundaries, you can simply start by writing own how much each person in your life hurt you or make you feel uncomfortable. Once you have identify your boundary issues, then consider the motivation behind each person's actions. The next step is to determine what actions you will take – you must be careful with the way you present your case, if someone's smoking habit is violating your boundary for instance you can simply tell him "I will really appreciate your help not to smoke while you are with me" do not use straightforward command requests such as "Do not smoke whenever you are with me". You need to remember the importance of saying a polite "No" to any request from time to time, especially when the other person is aware of your new boundaries. Try as much as possible to stop using humors in putting other people down.

The "Five things" technique of resetting personal boundaries

- o List the most important five things you want people to stop doing around you every day.

- o List the most serious things you want people to stop doing to you, for instance list some nicknames you want people to stop calling you or lists negative thoughts people normally have about you – for instance " You always give up easily" , " You have a bad breadth".

The second stage is; think about your current boundaries, and then ask the following questions;

- o How much attention do people around you expect from you at a moment (your family. Friends and co-workers, etc.) ?

- o Do you always make yourself available always? For instance; do you always answer phone calls even when you are always busy?

- o How much praise do you receive when you do something extra-ordinarily?

- o Why are you so popular with your friends?

- o How do you feel when you spend time with each member of your family or each of your friends?

Re-defining or re-adjusting your boundaries means you have to get yourself out of the mentality of pleasing other, to doing what is just.

Chapter 14
Common boundary myths

By now, you should be able to understand the importance of setting boundaries for both personal and relationship growth. Many individuals will struggle to set and maintain boundaries because of some myths and because they are afraid of the consequences such boundaries can have on their values and their lifestyle- for instance, some people are afraid of losing all their friends when their boundaries seem to be too high and unrealistic. It is important to deal with certain common boundary myths and embrace reality, in order to set boundaries successfully.

Myth #1: I may appear selfish if I set boundaries

This myth or objection is often raised by individuals who think or feared being considered as selfish or self-centered when they set boundaries. Many people are afraid of being accused of lacking concerns for others when they set boundaries, hence they give up setting such boundaries. In reality, setting boundaries does not make you selfish, setting boundaries as a matter of fact will help you take care of others, while you protect yourself from being at the receiving end of every misgivings. People who set the most limits are usually the most caring ones in the world and the reason for this is that they have discovered that through boundaries, their own needs have been taken care of, hence they have plenty of time and energy to take care of the needs of others.

We all have needs, desires, and selfishness only consider our own desires, whereas boundaries consider our needs. When we focus on our desires, we may lose focus and balance, and instead of pursuing our healthy goals through setting boundaries, selfishness may force us to work to satisfy others. Trying to meet our needs does not make such needs bad.

Myth #2: Boundaries are symptoms of disobedience and un-submissiveness

Many people are afraid that setting boundaries or limits will signal to their partners, colleagues, friends or bosses that they are rebellious and disobedient in nature. Some people believe that saying "No" to something good simply means they are unresponsive, hence they participate in every social gathering, or take whatever that is thrown at them. Doing everything that comes your way has no emotional or spiritual value. When you do things out of sense of duty, but your heart is not in it, then you are wasting your time and trying to please others. Focus on setting boundaries in whatever you do so that you don't do too much.

Outwardly obliging to something when we actually mean No simply makes you a liar, and if we say no to good things just because of our selfish desires, then such a boundary makes you disobedient.

Myth #3: Setting boundaries means I am always angry

For most beginners who are just setting boundaries, they may realize that they suddenly begin to tell the truth and take responsibilities for all their actions. These people may feel that they are being surrounded by some form of "anger cloud", most especially when they become sensitive to where their boundaries are being violated. When you start setting boundaries, you may fear that you can become easily offended, and this may get you confused. This is just one of the things you may experience at the onset of boundary setting but you will definitely get over it, when people start to understand what you stand for. Boundaries does not cause anger in us, however, if you see boundary setting as the source of your anger, then you are misunderstanding your emotions. Your emotions should be the signals that should notify you about something – for instance, your fear should tell you to move away from a dangerous situation, while anger should tell you to challenge an imminent threat.

You should take note that an angry situation is a warning that you are in an imminent danger of being attacked or injured. For this reason, anger should be seen as a positive sign that you are about to be manipulated, or your boundary is about to be violated. While your fear may tell you to withdraw from a situation, anger will definitely help you step forward and protect your boundary. There is no reason to be frightened when your boundaries are being violated, rather, the anger should help you engage in a reasonable but not violent way to tell the violator to stop violating your boundaries.

Don't just let your anger out, rather you should learn to protect whatever is yours in a more proper manner without showing negative emotions.

Myth #4: When I start creating boundaries, I may be hurt by others

It is often complicated when you set boundaries with people who do not respect limitations. It is true that many people don't like it when we present our opinions and arguments, and may get angry at us or simply withdraw from associating with us but this does not mean you should treat people softly always because they don't respect your boundary. You must not refrain from the truth, because those who love the truth will find it easier to associate with you. It is more important to be loved by few who understand the truth, than to be hated by many who want to oppress and take advantage of you.

Ask yourself the question; what if the person who hates you for your boundaries is your spouse? Will you then comply with no boundary rules just to protect the peace in your relationship? Or will you just endure his bad sides and let him violate your boundaries and still walk out on you. If you are afraid of the survival of your relationship and keep allowing your spouse to treat you badly, then you may not have the courage to set the boundaries. It is ideal to discover the hidden true character of your spouse and resolve all necessary issues instead of avoiding the problem.

It is very likely that you will get hurt from setting boundaries, but it is even much more likely that your relationship will become deeper.

Myth #5: When I set boundaries I may hurt others

You may end up disappointing other people occasionally when you set boundaries, especially when you value the happiness of such people. Some of the cases where you may hurt people when you set boundaries include;

- When a friend wants to borrow your car when you need it,

- People may call you for a social gathering preparation , and that is when you are physically down, or

- When a relative gets into a difficult financial situation but you can't loan him the exact amount because you have some financial obligations to take care of too.

Depending on how you see boundaries, you may hurt or may not hurt others, but nothing can be better than knowing the truth and the truth is that setting boundaries around your treasures are the only way you can protected them from being taken, destroyed or trampled upon. When you set boundaries for the wrong purpose or motive, then you may hurt the right people, but you need to keep in mind that saying No for the right reason will not cause injury to other people, even though it may cause discomfort and they have to look elsewhere for the same favor.

It is not your responsibility to meet the needs of everyone, though you should do everything possible to help others achieve their goals (but not at the detriment of your own happiness). You should help others freely when you have the resources to do so, and even when someone dare to you have a problem, you may have other more serious issues to contend with, hence you must attempt to solve the most important issues in your own life before considering meeting the needs of others. Sometimes you may be the one who gets turned down, hence you need to develop some supportive relationships where you do not become enslaved because of others.

Myth #6: Boundaries may become difficult to accept

Some people are afraid of setting up boundaries because of bad experiences they had in the past regarding past boundaries that were set on them. Getting yourself to accept the boundaries set by others can become unpleasant. Since nobody likes to be turned down, you need to prepare your mind for negative answers you get when you cross the boundaries set by others. You may ask yourself; why is it difficult for people to accept boundaries?

- During your childhood, you might have been injured by certain inappropriate boundaries set by people. When parents set boundaries around their children for instance, the children may feel some sense of not being wanted and this may follow them through their adulthood, and often feel unaccepted when the word "No" is said to them. The good news is that old bad news don't have to stick in your memory especially when you learn to accept other people's boundaries.

- Individuals who were deeply hurt by boundaries in their childhood often try to escape from the hurt by meeting the same boundaries against others. Setting limits on other people cannot allow you impost hatred on them because they will simply walk away from you for the right reason. Never project your old feelings from the boundaries set on you, on your children, friends, colleagues and other people around you.

- Inability to accept boundaries set by others, especially in your marital life, may tend to do with your intentions of cheating on your spouse. If your emotional satisfaction will always depend on your spouse's being on your side at all time, then something is not right about the relationship because you are the only one who set boundaries.

- Failure to accept boundaries may mean someone has problems in taking responsibilities. Sometimes, many people are accustomed to relying on people to rescue them from problems they deliberately brought on themselves, these people think the responsibilities of their own wellbeing are in the hands of others, hence they feel dejected when such obligations are not met by their beneficiaries. When you learn to take responsibilities for your own life, you will be confident of setting boundaries.

Myth #7: Boundaries may result in feelings of guilt

This is another myth many people can't comprehend, the reason being that the feeling of obligation may become an obstacle for them in setting boundaries that can be beneficial. It is difficult to say No to someone who has helped us in the past, especially with money, efforts and time. All you need to do is give gratitude for what has been done to you, instead of feeling guilty for setting boundaries. Many of us are not comfortable with taking free gifts because we always believe sometime we have to pay something back in return, and some people don't want to accept gifts any longer because they don't want to worry about paying back in the future.

Some people do not give selflessly, however they give for the purpose of needing us in the future, and you can tell the difference between these people by the way they react even after you thank them for their gesture- Kind givers don't even wait for you to thank them because they expect nothing from you. If the giver is angered by doing you a favor, then the person see the gift as an investment, and if the gratitude you offer is enough, then he or she probably wants nothing in return.

The issue of gratitude and boundaries must be kept separate, because boundaries must not be nullified because of gratitude, hence this myth holds no weight.

Myth #8: Boundaries will separate me from others

Many people are afraid of setting up personal boundaries because they are afraid of becoming social outcasts or appearing different from others- these people tend to avoid anything that may make them seem different from everyone else. You need to understand that going with the crowd always will rob you of your individuality, even if it will make tings different from you. You need to understand that you have a free-will and responsibility for yourself and those entrusted in your care, hence you must set boundaries in order to protect whatever is treasurable to you. It is your responsibility to decide the choices you want for your life and you don't have to become a puppet for someone to trample on you. Your relationship with the crowd must have limit, hence your boundaries must be completely under your control. When you discover that your property line will be respected, then you can re-adjust your boundaries (for instance, make it less tough). Boundaries will make you different and people will eventually learn to separate and respect you when they see how differently you do things.

Myth #9: Boundaries will become permanent and may create a permanent gap between me and others

Do not be deceived; there is nothing like a permanent boundary and the reason being that situations change, hence you have to change likewise. Many people believe that once boundaries are set, they can never be removed, they believe that boundaries will create a permanent gap between them and their friends, family and colleagues. You should learn to adjust your boundaries to current realities and situation; hence you wouldn't appear to be a difficult person.

Boundaries are not created to eliminate closeness; rather they create stronger bonds and more responsibilities. Boundaries will definitely lead to personality maturity and also help create the kind of closeness we deserve as humans. Naturally, immature people will want to stay away from us when we create boundaries, but they return to their senses when they see the true meaning of why you set such boundaries.

All the boundary misconceptions highlighted above should be regarded as mere misconceptions, true boundaries should be able to help you stand for yourself and say No to irresponsible activities.

Personal Boundary- Common difficulties you may face

Boundaries, especially when they are personal, can provide the freedom and growth that you desire. Setting up boundaries are not easy, likewise complying with such boundaries are even more difficult. You need to keep in mind that the purpose of setting boundaries is to protect yourself from bad influences. There are quite a number of ways of explaining the problems of setting and complying with boundaries, these are;

- •Compliance to boundaries may simply mean saying "Yes" to the bad things. This also means that the boundary setter may fail to set the limits and may continue to feel guilty of being controlled by others.

- •Avoidance of boundaries may simply means, one is saying No to the Good. The avoidant of a boundary may decide to close the gate of their love and affection of others.

- Failing to stay under control simply means one is failing to recognize the "No" of others. The controller in this case will try as much as possible to violate the boundaries set by others through manipulative and aggressive means.

- •Unresponsiveness to boundaries simply means the failure of the unresponsive individual to love others. Unresponsive people will naturally fail to hear about the needs and desires of others; hence they fail to give responsibility to care and help.

You don't have to comply with everything thrown at you, if you do, you will end up carrying the burdens of others, however controllers on the other hand want others to carry their burdens. Avoidant will generally want to shoulder their own burdens because they don't feel like seeking help from people. The non-responsive people will naturally refuse to help others even when the burdens of others' are becoming unbearable.

There are four major problems associated with personal boundaries and some people may develop problems in many of these areas at the same time. Boundary problems are;

○ Compliance,

○ Avoidance

○ Other-control, and

○ Unresponsiveness.

Compliance a major problem in boundary setting

Compliance is the number one and most prominent problems faced by people outside of a boundary set for them. Compliance is often the most difficult problem of boundary that can be tackled. Simply put, compliance in boundary is the difficulty to say No to others. We live in a conflicting world and if we don't learn to say words like "I disagree", "It hurts", and "That is wrong", we may find it difficult to survive the evils of this world. Many women are trained to be submissive and obedient and by doing such, they think they are inferior to men. Those who comply to boundaries often give-in to the demands of others in other to avoid to accept conflicts and that can force them to be subjected to manipulative and controlling people. It is not ideal to accept any abusive situation. When you are not submissive then you may influence the other person to change from his or her ways and embrace the truth.

Compliance as a problem in boundary setting may happen for a number of reasons, these include;

- The fear of hurting the feelings of other people,

- Fear of losing friendship or being abandoned,

- Fear of receiving the punishment for other people's anger,

- Fear of being labeled as "Selfish", and

- Feeling of guilt.

Being over-critical about one's evaluation can force one to engage in self-condemning acts, and many people's consciences are so weak that they become easily manipulated.

Complaints are simply unstable, hence you can't rely on them to take a stand for a long time.

Avoidance – a problem of boundary setting

Boundary setting will help keep the evil out of reach and also allow us to embrace the good. Some people seem to have problems with this believe because they have set their boundaries as walls because they allow the boundaries to become a protection where nothing is allowed through- this means no one can reach out to them for good , and this could be a disaster.

Avoidant people who set boundaries deliberately scare of people who want to reach out to them and care for them. Individuals who suffer from avoidance problems in boundary setting will always want to avoid people so that they wouldn't discover their needs. Avoidant deeply want someone to come to their rescue but the wall they created around themselves are too strong. Some individuals may also say that their issues cannot be compare to what others are dealing with, hence they want to resolve their problems by themselves.

Many men often try hard to ignore their emotional needs because they want to maintain a self-dependent strong image to people, they claim they possess everything they need and desire, whereas they are empty inside. Men don't want to be seen as weak. Some people who try to avoid conflicts are always drained in their own guilt of allowing others to use them for their selfish purpose, hence they constantly lose energy with nothing to replace it.

Control −a problem in boundary setting

Setting boundaries can be confusing and difficult; however, this can become a lot easier when people respect such boundaries. Some people always want to remain in control of others, and when we say No, they simply see as a challenge to change our minds- for instance, sales and market men and women, will always want to convince others to buy their products. Controllers will always have problems respecting the boundaries set by others. Controllers will try to use various means to get others shoulder their loads, and they usually come in two forms;

- Aggressive controllers, and

- Manipulative controllers.

Aggressive controllers are the most problematic people around because they do not care about other people's boundaries. Once they make up their mind, they simply want the whole world to be on their sides. They always want the final say, and they simply neglect their own responsibility and rely on others to handle them. Religious fanatics are good examples of aggressive controllers who do not care about boundaries set by others, but they want to impose their own beliefs and ideas on others.

Sometimes, we can only admire the traits of some aggressive controllers, especially when they put such qualities into good use.

Manipulative controllers are reasonable to certain extent in recognizing the boundaries set by others. Manipulative controllers will try to do everything possible to convince others to give up their boundaries, and they may often deny their desire to control others even though it is inherent that their final resort is to gain the attention and control of others for their selfish desires.

Most controllers often end up isolated but that doesn't mean they don't get to have people around them but they are unsure whether the people around them stay because of fear or dependency. If you are a controller who wants to manipulate others, then you need to confront your fear by giving up your control over others, otherwise you may end up losing respect and your boundary may be violated when you violate other people's boundaries.

Complaints and avoidant may also be controllers at the same time but they clearly state what their boundaries are.

Unresponsiveness- a problem in boundary setting

Unresponsiveness describe an attitude where some people live their own lives without bordering about the welfare of the people around them. Unresponsive people believe that life is tough and everyone needs to handle his or her own business. Unresponsive people often appear as if they are not distracted by things happening around them, as long as they accomplish whatever they have in mind. While unresponsiveness may thrive when setting boundaries in the business world, lack of sensitivity in marriage is a different case because it makes other partners appear cold, and such may lead to the disintegration of the relationship.

Unresponsive individuals will naturally shrug off the needs of others when they express such needs, and for unresponsive people, needs are simply distractions and nothing more. Unresponsive people believe they are not responsible for how others live their lives, and they don't feel the need to stay connected to the people around them or even help them shoulder part of their responsibilities.

Unresponsiveness in boundary setting may become even more complicated when individuals involved are also indulging in aggressive or manipulative control behavior. Individuals who are unresponsive and controlling at the same time never see beyond themselves, however, these people often find it extremely hard to get out of their problems because there might be no one to come around to help them due to their isolated lifestyles. In-completeness is usually the most striking features of individuals who suffer from unresponsive behavior especially when setting their own boundaries, they may appear to be satisfied with what they have when actually they are empty an lack happiness within.

It is important to start dealing with problems associated with boundary setting whenever they start to show up, this will help in identifying areas where you will need help and you wouldn't end up isolating yourself just because you have created a wall around you. The more boundary you set, the more problems you may actually face, hence it is advisable to keep boundaries to a manageable number at a time so that you can easily identify violators and also re-adjust realistically. In this case you may require some periodic evaluation of the performance or effect of the boundaries you set.

Chapter 15
Importance and benefits of setting boundaries as a leader

There is no doubt about the fact that the primary reason why a leader must set boundaries around himself is to ensure that duties are delegated to his subordinates so that they can become self-sufficient, self-reliant, and effective. Secondly, setting limits as a leader will ensure that realistic expectations are set for yourself, and you do not end up trying to do too much and end up achieving much less than your desired result. With a realistic boundary, you are able to control your actions as well as the results you want to get. Leaders who fail to set boundaries always want to achieve too many things at the same time and end up making too numerous mistakes.

Another benefit of setting boundaries is that; as a leader, setting boundaries will help you provide a solid structures for your subordinates to follow. A structure is simply a clear direction to which certain tasks must be completed, for instance; you can set boundaries on the inter-relations between company workers and clients, and any staff who violate such boundaries will be punished for doing so. When structures are set, certain tasks or goals can be achieved much faster and easier, however, when staffs do not have specific structures, they do things awkwardly and end up coming to ask you for help. A structure will ensure that your subordinates or followers are on the same page with you, so that you can achieve the final results within the time frames required.

Boundaries help in clarifying different roles. Without boundaries, there may be duplication of roles and such issues can create problems because it reduces productivity and even lead to loss in valuable time. When you clarify roles and provide different job description to each and every one under you, staffs will become motivated and they end up doing their specific tasks, hence less errors are committed and as the leader, you can easily correct any error because you can trace them to a specific individual or team.

Boundaries help leaders in tracing source of errors much faster. When you trace errors quickly, you can easily provide solutions to such errors, however, when you fail to set boundaries to the roles of each person, you may find it difficult to track errors committed, hence finding solutions to problems become more complicated. You need to set job descriptions alongside minimum baseline results you expect in order to achieve your goals and objectives as a leader.

Boundaries are goal-oriented. As a leader, you must avoid setting boundaries for selfish reasons because you may not achieve your aims and objectives in such manner. When you set boundaries for the common goals of the organization, you will become more satisfied with results achieved. When you fail to set boundaries, you will find it difficult to measure success because you don't have a minimum base-line for measuring such success.

One of the most powerful tools of boundary setting is measurement, it helps you evaluate how effective your boundaries are and where you need to make adjustments in order to achieve even better results. The more you measure and evaluate your goals and objectives, the more loopholes and errors you detect, hence you can become more confident that you are achieving your desired results.

Chapter 16
Types of boundaries you need to set as a leader

As a leader of an organization or group, there are quite a number of boundaries you must consider setting, these include;

- Job responsibility boundaries- these include Individual job responsibilities and team responsibilities.

- •Inter-personal boundaries- These include the interaction between co-workers as well as managers within the organization.

- Personal boundaries- These include some personal and special boundaries.

Job responsibility boundaries

As a leader, you need to set professional boundaries that should be based on the functions of each staff within the organization. Setting job responsibilities will ensure that each and every one is accountable to his or her duties and will reduce chances of laying blames on others for not completing individual responsibilities. Personal job responsibilities will prevent a staff from blaming another for poor job performance.

Employees need to understand their specific roles, and you must set boundaries on how staffs can help each other complete their tasks. You need to set boundaries for monitors or supervisors or whoever each staff reports to. You need to let each staff understand when he or she is pushing the boundaries, and he or she must know the right way to say No, or when to ask for what he or she needs without breaking the boundaries of other staffs. Borrowing of each other's' tools also fall under this category – there must be a limit to which a staff can borrow or use tools belonging to another.

Inter-personal boundaries

It is important to negotiate inter-personal boundaries at work place, in addition to job responsibilities, and the reason being that professional and Inter-personal boundaries determine to a large extent, make huge impacts on the productivity and quality of life within the work place. There are certain things you must consider when setting inter-personal boundaries at work place, these include;

- The type of tone people use with one another when conversing,

- The type of attitude co-workers use when interacting with each other at work,

- The ability of staffs to focus on their responsibilities within a team even when they bear personal grudges with any member of such team.

- The ability to set boundaries for individuals who have poor boundaries, and defining the consequences for each boundary broken.

As a leader, some of the personal boundaries you can set include; limiting the non-work related conversations such as social issues, sex-related conversations, and there must be no discussions on wages and salaries or the hanging of offensive religious images. Inter-personal boundaries are set to ensure higher productivity. As a leader, inter-personal boundaries must not be too weak otherwise you will be disturbed with allegations and accusations of workplace bullying. As a leader, you need to sect boundaries for yourself too otherwise your co-workers may become disrespectful, they may become or act needy and all these may devour the much needed energy and dedication to drive success.

Personal boundaries

Setting personal boundaries for yourself and others can boost the emotional state of each and every one and this can result in higher productivity. Technological advancements has made it easier for employees to have different modes of communication, an such high-tech gadgets may ease pressure at work place, but they may become abused hence, once of your priorities here is to avoid round-the-clock use of communication gadgets, it is better to limit the use of such devices to lunch time or after the close of work for the day. Productivity can diminished when staffs are not restricted when it comes to personal boundaries, likewise a leader needs to set boundaries on his closeness to subordinates and other managers.

You need to be flexible with all forms of boundaries you set, this will ensure that you are able to identify the loopholes in such boundaries and ways to improve them. Being flexible with boundaries does not mean you must weaken such boundaries, rather it helps you learn more about the response of people to such boundaries.

Chapter 17
How to set boundaries as a leader

There are five basic steps you need to take when setting boundaries as a leader and these are;

- Provide a boundary setting structure

- Clarify roles for yourself and others

- Set motivating roles,

- Give and provide feedbacks, and

- Evaluate your boundaries

Provide a boundary setting structure

Just like a home builder who starts the building of a house starting with a foundation, you need to create a baseline for your boundaries. A boundary structure will help you define the direction to which your boundaries are going. A leader with no clear direction cannot set boundaries, hence he may find it difficult to control everyone around him. Setting clear boundaries start with having clear direction, hence you need an ideal planning before setting your boundary structure. The more time you invest in your structure, the more solid your boundaries become.

You need good communication skills to set your boundary structure, because you need to communicate effectively with others and let them see reasons why boundaries are essential in the survival of an organization or entity for which you are a leader. You need to communicate your expectations clearly if you want people to take you serious as a leader. Some boundaries can be counter-intuitive if they are not properly considered and evaluated before they are set. With a structure, you will have a vision for the future. With a structure, you will be sure that everyone is on the same page towards the achievement of a common goal and objective.

Setting clear boundaries also involves defining everything within the scope of duties and what is not, such structure must also define the appropriate behaviors required from each person. Sometimes, setting boundaries will make you feel bossy and imposing, but they will soon realize that setting boundaries will actually empower them to become leaders and independent. With adequate structure for your boundaries, you will be able to train others to become innovative and initiative, hence they don't have to rely on you to make certain critical decisions for the good of an organization.

Clarify roles for yourself and others

You cannot set realistic boundaries without first making clarifications on the roles of each person within an entity. As the leader , everyone expect you to have leadership roles, including the general supervisory and management roles , however you need to consider the specific roles and job descriptions of each staff in each organization. As the leader, you need to check whether the work other staffs are doing actually match the job descriptions they are hired to do, then you can set boundaries in order to correct such errors. You need to check whether the job descriptions are appropriate for the boundary structures that you have set already.

Generally you should expect that each staff's current jobs will match between 50% and 99% of their job descriptions. For this reason, staffs will need to adapt when the priorities have finally shifted. You need to keep in mind as a leader that the job descriptions of other staffs are the baseline for which boundaries can be set. As a leader, you need to encourage others to seek career development, and the best way they can do that is to avoid violating boundaries.

Set motivating roles

It is ideal to set goals right when setting boundaries. When goals align with an organization's goals, then it will be easier for staffs to avoid violating boundaries, no matter how difficult such boundaries are. Motivating goals will help staffs put all their energy and mind in following ethics and avoid violating boundaries. It is easy to become stressed out when work piles up and there are no limits or boundaries guiding you and others on what should be done at a specific time of the day. When you don't set priorities or boundaries, it is very easy to lose track, hence boundaries help you stay focused and in the right lane.

Goals must make a difference in people's lives before they can motivate them to achieve the collective goals and aspirations of an organization. There must be a measurable achievement attached to boundaries, and that is how such boundaries can motivate people to achieve their goals and dreams. You need to make the boundaries set make the difference between success and failure clear so that people can avoid violating such boundaries. The completion of each goal must always evoke some sense of pride in your followers.

Give and provide feedbacks

You need to keep in mind that no one is perfect, hence you should leave room for the violation of boundaries, however, it must not be rampant. People find it difficult to adjust to new rules and changes, hence keeping to boundaries can be difficult at the beginning. In order to ensure a continued improvement in keeping to boundaries, you need to engage in conversations. When you seek an honest conversation and accept feedbacks from others, then you must provide your own feedback to ensure that you reach agreements. Just because you set boundaries does not mean you must be defensive always.

Evaluate your boundaries

Evaluating your boundaries in order to determine their effectiveness is important. There is no point setting boundaries when no one is respecting them, hence you need to know when to get tougher on violators of boundaries. Evaluating your boundaries will help you explore their strength and weaknesses and areas where you need to make minor adjustments.

Chapter 18
Common problems or challenges faced when setting boundaries as a leader

There must be consequences established when job, personal or inter-personal boundaries are related, however, there are certain situations under which issues are left to the discretion of leaders, especially when there are no consequences set against the violation of certain boundaries or when boundaries were not established in certain situations. As a leader, you must provide each employee with an organization's boundary manual where consequences must be clearly stated, and each consequence must measure according to the severity of each violation. Violation of boundaries relating to sexual harassment, physical abuses, mental abuses, and lying must not be tolerated in any manner.

Some of the commonest problems associated with boundary setting for leaders are;

- Lack of implementation of consequences,

- Setting weak boundaries

- Boundary rejection

- Ignorance towards boundaries, and

- Use of boundaries for aggressive control or power.

Lack of implementation of consequences for boundary violation

Sometimes leaders do not clearly understand some of the boundaries they set, hence they set the wrong punishment for certain boundaries. When you do not conduct a thorough research on the boundaries you set, you may end up setting the right boundaries for the wrong purpose or even punish someone unjustly for violating the wrong boundary. You need to weight your options and consider communicating with your subordinates before implementing certain boundaries and their consequences. You need to consult other managers or leaders before setting boundaries , and they can give you the appropriate consequences to put in place- these are consequences that will not violate company's goals and objectives as well as the right of other co-workers.

Setting weak boundaries

It is better not to set boundaries at all than set weak boundaries that you can hardly enforce. When your boundaries are weak, they are easier to violate, and you may never be taken seriously even when you change or upgrade the boundaries. All possible loopholes in your boundaries must be blocked to ensure that co-workers do not explore such weaknesses for their own selfish gains. Boundaries should not be enforced until they have been tested and proven to be in accordance with the organization's goals and objectives. Weak boundaries must not be implemented until they have been strengthened in order to ensure there are no confusion.

Boundary rejection

Certain boundaries by leaders can be misconstrued by co-workers, especially when they see it as a sudden show of force or aggressiveness towards their interests. Boundary rejection is one of the most prominent issues associated with boundary settings for leaders and it must be discouraged, otherwise it could lead to chaos, strike actions and protests that may reduce productivity and even cost an organization its reputation. Boundary rejection may also occur when someone perceived to be the victim believes that the boundaries are not included in an organization's rules and standards or ethics. It is important for leaders to understand the likelihood of boundaries being rejected especially when the rights of co-workers are violated or when such boundaries were not communicated earlier on.

Ignorance towards boundaries

Some co-workers understand that certain boundaries exist however, they may show lackadaisical attitude toward such boundaries for certain reasons. Some co-workers may have personal hatred towards leaders, while some deliberately violate such boundaries to proof a point. In some cases, Ignorance toward certain boundaries occur when the punishment for violating such boundaries are too weak or do not exist. Ignorance towards legitimate boundaries must be treated as a serious issue and consequences must be applied appropriately, otherwise perpetrators of such acts may influence others to indulge in it too. A co-worker may deliberately ignore boundaries if he feels his personal, mental or health conditions were not considered before such boundaries were implemented.

Use of boundaries for aggressive control or power

As a leader, it is morally wrong to use boundaries to impose certain boundaries because you want to exercise your authority and force over others. Leaders with egos are usually found using boundaries to control or influence others in work places. A leader for instance may impose certain boundaries in order to force employees to obey certain orders, especially when such orders are not part of an organization's ethics or standards. Some leaders may use urgent or sudden boundaries to punish some staffs who are unruly or who report them. Aggressive boundaries may also be set for personal reasons, especially when a leader believes his subordinates are not giving their best or performing at the optimal capacity and targets were not being met.

Some aggressive boundaries may be necessary when workers attitudes to work are hampering the growth and development of the organization, though, these orders may be ideal but must be implemented cautiously to avoid uncontrollable damages and losses.

Chapter 19
Tackling common boundary issues as a leader

No matter how good you are as a leader, you need to set boundaries to avoid your personal space being violated and to ensure that motivate orders to work as a team, complete orders and maintain high productivity that will lead the organization to the height of its expectations. There are numerous boundary issues you will face as a leader and your ability to resolve such issues will either make or mare your career, hence the issue of setting boundaries must be handled with caution.

Once you have identify the need for boundaries as a leader, it is important to incorporate such boundaries into your own goals and aspirations, and you must recognize the fact that such personal leadership boundaries are not rigid barriers but strict guidelines to certain behaviors and relationships. There are a number of ways through which you can establish boundaries successfully as a leader and avoid conflicts whether at work, home or in social circuits;

- Draw clear and distinct boundaries between your work time and family- Great leaders know how to balance work demands with family and social responsibilities, hence they set boundaries based on their work, family and social needs and ensure that such boundaries do not create conflicts. When you are not working you should force yourself to do away with certain gadgets and devices, these include; pagers, laptops , and cellphones – you can leave these gadgets at home to ensure that you pay maximum attention to your family and stay connected with everyone.

Secondly, try as much as possible to make necessary plans such as vacations well ahead of time, by doing this, you will ensure that all plans are scheduled on your calendar. Great leaders always make plans ahead of time to avoid setting unrealistic boundaries.

- Be flexible with your boundaries- Being flexible is an essential attitude towards setting leadership boundaries because your co-workers will be more proactive and respectful when you listen to their plights, and challenges, however this does not mean you must create weak boundaries. For instance, when you are on a team working hard to complete a task and your co- workers see you working beyond time schedules, they will be motivated to stay longer on certain days with you just to ensure that tasks are completed. Being flexible does not mean you must allow everyone violate boundaries, rather

- learn to change yourself as a leader- setting boundaries start with learning to change yourself. You can't change anyone else when you are not open to personal changes. Hence you need to set boundaries for yourself first before setting boundaries for others. Self -improvement is important if we want others to respect our boundaries, and it is not right to presume that others will respect your boundaries or turn off yourself when just because you want to preserve your own freedom.

- Be willing to accept other people's boundaries- respect is always reciprocal, and when you respect other people's boundaries, they will do the same for you.

Accepting other people's boundaries does not mean you have to lower your standards and allow everyone to take control of you. Certain boundaries are set by others to influence the decisions made by the rest or aggressively used in taking control of others.

- Communication is the key to avoiding boundary conflicts- One of the main reasons why people ignore or disrespect boundaries is lack of communication. When boundaries are set hurriedly, there are bound to be conflicts because others are not aware of such boundaries in the first place, and when you impose consequences for such actions, they will simply see you as an aggressor and will withdraw respect for you. You don't want to isolate yourself with unrealistic boundaries, hence you must communicate effectively as a leader, to your subordinates and make sure that you receive their protests before setting consequences.

- Feedbacks are necessary when setting boundaries because they help you identify areas that need to be improved and boundaries that are unrealistic towards achieving your goals. There are several ways through which you can get feedback on certain boundaries; you can conduct personal interview sessions with individuals to be affected by your boundaries, or through surveys and questionnaires. The more feedbacks you get, the more information you can retrieve to ensure that your boundaries are realistic and can be effective on a long term.

- As a leader, you need to realize that good boundaries will lead to good relationships- as a leader, you need to train others how you want them to treat you. By communicating your limits to people you create mutual respect. You need to stop and ponder on what you want and what you want to happen, and then you can work-out how boundaries can help you achieve such aspirations.

- Your tasks and responsibilities- To certain extent, your tasks and responsibilities will depend on others. You will naturally be expected to fulfill your own responsibilities but keep in mind that some un-expected situations will always show up, hence you must set up boundaries to ensure that you don't end up saying yes to everything thrown your way.

- The expectation of others- as a leader, much is expected from you, hence you must be prepared to lead by example to avoid boundary related conflicts. You need to remember that at certain times, you will fall sick and unable to perform some of your leadership roles, but when you are flexible with your boundaries, others will be willing to lift you up because you also help them when they are down and unable to perform their duties.

- Any boundary that is counter-productive against your leadership position or the overall interest of an organization, must be withdrawn and re-examined immediately before it is too late.

- Boundaries are collective responsibilities of each and every one, hence you are not the only one who should monitor violators, and you may delegate people to perform such monitoring tasks.

Chapter 20
Real reasons why you need to set boundaries early dating

There are so many reasons you should consider for setting boundaries early in dating and primary one is that you don't want to lose your value and respect.

One of the main reasons why some couples are afraid of setting boundaries in relationships is that they are afraid of losing their partner, thus they keep accommodating insults and disrespect. You need to transform yourself from a "door mat" to someone with value, in order to become respected. When you start learning to set boundaries at the early stages of dating, your partner may tell you that you have become weird or changed, however he or she has simply become upset for not being able to throw any dirt at you any longer.

Setting boundaries earlier in dating is not manipulative and controlling.

Many people also believe that the main reasons couples start setting boundaries in a relationship is when one wants to start manipulating or controlling the other. This could be true for some people but genuine boundaries should not turn you to an aggressive controller in a relationship. When you set boundaries because you want to have absolute control on every aspect of a relationship, your partner may become frustrated and the relationship may end, but when realistic boundaries are set, with respect to the feelings of your partner, he or she will reason with you and try to conform to such boundaries.

To protect your dignity, honesty and Integrity

When you are afraid of losing someone, then you will be afraid of setting boundaries but at the same time you should consider the fact that your integrity, dignity and honesty will be at risk. When you don't set boundaries in the early stages of dating, you are putting your integrity and dignity at risk because you are afraid of upsetting your partner. For instance, you are angry that your man is flirting with your friend but you are afraid of telling him to stop. When you are afraid of telling your partner to stop a bad habit then you are under his or her manipulation.

To own your strength and avoid giving your power to strangers

You may find it harder to love or forgive people, especially when you don't have the strength to set boundaries in your relationships. Your inability to set boundaries simply shows that you don't love yourself, and you need to have high self-esteem in order to possess enough strength and energy to set boundaries at the early stages of dating.

Your inability to set boundaries may result in losing trust, you will notice that trust in yourself and trust in others start to diminish when you don't have personal rules guiding you. If you can't trust yourself to have the backing of others, you will naturally keep people at distance from your space, and you may likely become obsessed about others taking advantage of you.

Anyone can mess with your heart when you don't trust yourself, therefore, you need to summon enough courage right now and start saying No to all negativities being thrown at you.

Have you noticed that the nicest people often become the angriest people? The reason for this is that they have lots of resentments towards others and constantly fight hard to express their dissatisfaction towards certain negative issues; hence their real attitudes are rarely seen because of their resentments toward others. Do not have resentment towards others because people will walk over you and ask you for more.

People who often show the fear of disapproval from people are always afraid to set boundaries. When you are not afraid of being disapproved, people will suddenly have respects for you and will definitely don't want to cross your boundaries because they know the consequences.

Without rules people will trample on your dignity and will always take your feelings for granted because they know you are too weak to act.

Chapter 21
Transitioning from "doormat" person to someone with boundaries and rules

In order to learn to set boundaries at the early stages of dating, you need to develop your mind and body, especially when you have been suffering from low self-esteem in the past.

The best possible way to transition from a "doormat" person into a person of incredible strength is to start slowly. If you are currently dating someone, you don't have to start setting rules or boundaries by blasting him or her with so many rules, doing otherwise will make you appear mean and possessive. You need to start by slowly integrating your partner into the relationship and boundaries. If you are just starting a relationship it is better to write down the rules as early as possible, however such rules will still have to be evaluated and adjusted in such a way that your partner's feelings, strength and weaknesses must be considered before the boundaries are finally set.

Write out the things you wouldn't tolerate from your partner, for instance you can arrange such rules as follows;

- The only positive energy allowed in this relationship is love and respect,

- When you treat me with respect, I will do the same unto you,

- Be nice to me or be gone from me,

- If you can't relax and talk to me in a calm manner then you must calm down before we engage in a talk.

- Honesty, compassion and Integrity are non-negotiable in this relationship.

You will likely become scared and nervous when you notice for the first time that someone has violated your boundaries. Don't expect much from yourself when standing up against your partner who is violating your boundaries for the first time; simply tell him or her about it- it takes time for people to get used to new rules.

Over time, more practice will help you get used to enforcing boundaries and it will become even easier for your partner to recognize your boundaries, hence you don't have to repeat yourself from time to time especially when he or she is aware of the consequences of violating such rules.

You need to learn to stick with the boundaries set by your partner, in as much as you want him or her to obey your boundaries. Practice make perfect but communication is even more important- you need to communicate with your partner , ahead of enforcing boundaries , the reason being that certain boundaries may cause physical or emotional harm , hence such boundaries may not be realistic. Setting boundaries should be a two-way process, you must allow your partner review such rules before enforcing them.

Chapter 22
Boundary setting principles to adopt when setting dating boundaries

Setting boundaries can be difficult at the beginning, however, the modern day dating requires boundaries at all cost in other to sustain such relationships on a long term. Your relationship must not be based on physical affection only; it must be made strong in order to make it survive all forms of challenges.

Principle one: The "S" word

Most boundaries often revolve around Sex and other related issues. Sexual activities are inevitable in any dating, however, if not handled properly, it can make or break the relationship. While certain boundaries should be set around sexual activities, you must not use sex as a form of punishment when your partner violates your boundaries. Se in dating should be for intimacy, procreation and pleasure, and must not be used as a weapon against a partner. You need to be careful when setting boundaries around se, you need to be sure about what is acceptable to you and what is acceptable to your partner so that you wouldn't end up hurting each other.

Sex-related boundaries must be emphatically created to stop extra-marital activities, and by setting these boundaries you must have a clear agreement with your spouse on certain sex related issues, including the frequencies of having intimacy and intercourse. Any medical condition interfering with intimacy must be discussed to ensure that it does not cause problems later in the future.

Principle two: How far do you want to go in the relationship?

Not all dating require long term boundaries, as a matter of fact, you need to be sure whether you want to enter into a short or long term relationship with your partner before setting boundaries. Secondly, you need to consider the issue – How far is too far? There are certain boundaries that need to be measured because you are unsure about how far you want such boundaries to go. You need to draw the lines around certain boundaries, for instance; sexual intercourse (you need to know the extent or frequency of such activities).

In a committed relationship, you need to allow your conscience to guide you in setting boundaries, when you are guided by your conscience, you will be able to set boundaries according to the commitment of the other person (either he or she wants a long term commitment or a short term relationship). There is no point setting boundaries for someone you are not sure will stay with you for a long time. You need to ask your partner how far he or she wants to go before setting any boundary.

Principle three: Do not say Yes when you mean No

Nothing can be as confusing as saying No when you mean yes or vice versa. You must be affirmative with boundaries, if you want your partner to take you serious. Do not say No just to get the attention of your partner, and when you actually mean yes. You need to say Yes when you feel your needs are important, hence you must set boundaries that you mean and not for selfish reasons. Words such as "Its fine" or "whatever", are not affirmative, and must not be used when setting boundaries or communicating with your partner.

Principle four: Say what you want to say even if he or she doesn't want to listen

Voicing out your opinion or frustration should not be done in an aggressive manner, but it is a means of communication that helps your partner understand you even much easier. You don't have to be afraid of the reaction you will get from your partner, as long as your communicate with him in a positive way. Lack of communication is the primary course of most problems in setting boundaries in dating. When you want to set boundaries, your partner will expect some explanations for such boundaries before he or she will oblige.

Principle five: Boundary setting in dating is a "give and take" issue

A successful relationship is the one where a partner choose to sacrifice without expecting anything in return, however, when it comes to setting boundaries in dating, the principle of Give and take is important. Your partner will find it easier to accept your boundaries when you are prepared to accept his own, hence there wouldn't be conflict of interest.

You don't have to feel let-down because you remind your partner about a boundary that has been violated – for instance, if he repeatedly failed to turn up for a date on time. You don't have to tolerate certain behaviors for so long when you are dating, otherwise, your partner will continue to abuse such privileges. If you want to keep your dignity intact without compromising on your respect and value, you must expect a give-and-take situation when setting boundaries early in dating.

Chapter 23
Types of boundaries you must set early dating

Whether you are casually dating someone or you are serious about taking the relationship to another level, there are three main types of boundaries you must consider setting earlier in dating, these are;

- Emotional boundaries,

- Physical boundaries, and

- Digital boundaries.

Emotional boundaries

Emotional boundaries are the most important boundaries you must set as early as possible when dating someone, and the reason being that our emotions govern every decision we make, hence you don't want your emotions to misguide you when making critical decisions. Both partners need to understand each other's wants, needs and goals in order to make the relationship work out, and you need to feel free to communicate your feelings to your partner. Your partner should not get angry at you unnecessarily or without cause, and you must always feel safe, secured and transparent in your relationship.

The use of the "L" word in a relationship is non-negotiable because you must always say it to your partner. The word "Love" is the most assuring word in any relationship, and you need to let your partner knows how much it makes you feel and why he must mean it when he says it. Emotional boundaries should cover all aspect of dating; you don't want to see him or her flirting with your friends, hence you must let him or her know at the beginning. You may also let him or her know that you need to have the password to his or her smartphone, otherwise you must not bother about suspecting him or her each time his or her phone rings. Setting emotional boundaries will help build trust in a relationship.

The time you spent apart as partners can affect how effective your boundaries are. As good as it may sound to spend every time together with your partner, it's important that you also set aside certain time to spend apart- Researches has shown that partners who create time to spend apart will often appreciate themselves more than those who want to spend time always together. One of the boundaries you must set earlier in dating is making your partner realize when you need to spend time to do things on your own. You don't have to get trapped into doing things together always, as a matter of fact, the more time you spend alone, the more you discover about yourself and your partner.

Physical boundaries

Most physical boundaries created in dating are done to create space. Space invasion is one of the issues that cause problems in relationships most especially when one partner is always interested in knowing everything the other partner is doing. You don't want your partner to ask you where you have gone to or what you are doing presently when you are not together, hence you must not invade his privacies always. Couples need to be aware of each other's movements and aspirations but when it becomes too much of a habit, your partner may become easily irritated. You don't have to be in a rush when you are not ready. In a healthy relationship partners often know how far they want to go, hence they create boundaries in certain areas just to ensure that the future of their relationship is guaranteed.

Physical boundaries help couples stay disciplined, especially when they recognize that "Sex is not a currency", there is no rule that says that sex must come into a relationship at certain age or time, however taking your time in a relationship will help you ascertain when actually you are ready for intimacy. You need to set boundaries, especially when your partner is pressuring you into certain physical intimacy in your relationship, you need to be sure about your readiness.

Digital boundaries

Digital boundaries are the most complicated types of boundaries in relationships because it is extremely difficult to draw a line when your relationship gets online. The rules laid down by social media websites such as Facebook, Twitter, and Snapchat are not applicable to real life situations, and you need to set boundaries on how much of your personal information you can share online. Your partner must be aware of the digital boundaries you set so that you can limit the influence of others in your relationship. Just before you discuss your online relationships with your partner, you need to check the things that make your comfortable online.

You need to check the following digital boundaries in order to determine what works for you;

- Is it appropriate for you to check-in or tag certain people on your social media profiles?

- Do you and your partner have to post your relationship status online always? You need to remember the kind of problems you may face if you eventually breakup with your partner.

- Is it okay to follow your partner's friends or is it okay for your partner to add your friends?

- Is it okay for you to have access to your partner's social medial profile? And can you even post, commend or share contents on his or her behalf?

- Is it okay to send posts, tweets or even comment about your relationship?

You need to be cautious about setting boundaries when it comes to the issue of the influence of social media on your relationship. Once you have figure out what exactly you want, you can talk to your partner in order to create an ideal digital dating boundary, hence you can decide what is healthy and what is unhealthy, so that you wouldn't get hurt if you have to break up eventually. As you work out a beneficial dating boundary, there will likely be some compromises and negotiation as you figure out what works best for both of you. You need to set boundaries as regards digital or internet's influence on your relationship so that your partner wouldn't force you do what you are not comfortable doing.

Digital agreement and boundaries can be easily changed as your relationship progresses because you will continue to discover what is healthy and what is not. Just because you felt comfortable with certain things at the beginning of your relationship does not mean you will stick with such forever. Learning to communicate with your partner when things are changing will allow him or her to freely and openly communicate with you.

When you are contemplating digital boundaries, you should consider the following tips or principles;

- All digital passwords must be kept private- Even if you trust your partner very much, sharing passwords to your social media networks, your smartphone or any other digital device may not always be the best idea. You need to understand that you are entitled to your own digital privacy just as you are entitled to spend time by yourself. Giving your social media password and login details will give him or her opportunity of posting, sharing or commenting on certain issues without your permission.

  When you don't set digital boundaries, your partner will see everyone you communicate with and he or she may have access to some sensitive materials that may cause him or her to change attitude towards you. If you want to prevent unnecessary jealousy in your relationship, you need to have absolute control over your digital password. In order to be on the safe side, your password should remain your right and under your control.

- Photos- Many couples share photos recklessly online and many of these pictures often end up on the internet whether deliberately or otherwise. When sharing explicit pictures with your partner, you need to set boundaries because your partner may use such pictures against you when things go awry between the two if you. You need to

Chapter 24
Problems associated with boundaries in dating and how to tackle them

There are quite a lot of problems associated with setting boundaries at the onset of dating; however the most prominent among these problems are;

- Improper or poor boundaries,

- Setting boundaries for control or power,

- Lack of communication

- Irresponsiveness to boundaries, and

- Boundary rejection

Improper boundaries

Setting the right boundaries at the right time, or setting the wrong boundaries in dating can cause such boundaries to remain ineffective. Setting poor boundaries for your relationship can make you become predictable because everyone knows what you can do even if your partner violates your boundary. You need to be affirmative in the boundaries you set, hence you must be resolute and ensure that you stick with every decision you make. There is no point keeping your social media profile keywords for a while and later decide to give them out to your partner when you know what he is capable of doing. Try as much as possible to set long term boundaries that can be sustained.

Setting boundaries to control or power

Nothing can be more excruciating in a relationship than when a partner discovers that you have set certain boundaries in order to exercise control, or power over him or her. You must never make the mistake of trying to change your partner through your boundaries; similarly you must not try to manipulate him or her by setting unrealistic boundaries that you know he or she will never stick to. Boundaries are designed to help safeguard your interest in a relationship and not to become an aggressive controller over your partner, hence you must respect his or her feelings, goals and struggles before you set boundaries, and at the same time you need to know where the relationship is heading to.

Lack of communication

Setting boundaries do not end when they are set in relationships; proper communication is essential before, during and after you set the boundaries. When you don't tell your partner about your boundaries, he may violate such boundaries without even knowing. Similarly, you need to make clarifications on certain boundary issues so that you don't get your partner confused. Your partner need some explanation before you set boundaries so that he or she doesn't think you are deliberately trying to make things complicated. When you communicate the consequences of breaking certain boundaries, your partner will find ways not to break such boundaries. Some people don't like being reported to their parents, friends or colleagues when they don't do things in the proper way, hence you should rather communicate with him or her instead of reporting him to his or her parents and getting him or her upset.

Irresponsiveness to boundaries

One of the things that can frustrate the success of boundaries in dating is the non-responsiveness of a partner to boundaries. Some partners deliberately ignore boundaries because they are not comfortable with such and this could make a relationship complicated. When a partner refuses to respond to a boundary, it may mean that he or she will never respect the boundary or he or she does not care about the consequences of breaking such boundary- this may make the relationship become strained and the best option is to give such a person some time to grow and adjust to such boundaries or end the affair in order to avoid heartbreaks.

Boundary rejection

Boundary rejection is the worst problem you can expect when dating because it is a sign of incompatibility. Some partners may reject certain boundaries for the right reasons, especially when they believe such boundaries were set to exercise control or impose certain things that may violate their privacies, physical or emotional state. There should always be a time to review boundaries before they are finally presented before a partner, this will ensure that both parties agree and deliberate on all issues to avoid making the relationship become complicated. Boundary rejection could mean that your spouse has something to hide, especially when it comes to extra-marital affairs- an individual who always hide his phone from his or her partner will reject certain rules because he or she doesn't want to get caught.

Chapter 25
Why do you need to set boundaries with children?

The primary reason you need to set boundaries for your kids is to protect them from harm. For instance, teaching yourself the act of "self-defense" is a boundary your kid needs to know in order to protect himself from predators or bullies. Self-defense boundaries are not taught to make kids become rude; rather, you need to let them know when they supposed to use such skills only when they are in danger.

When most kids approach their first year birthday, most parents often struggle to set boundaries, many of such parents are afraid or too soft to tell kids about their boundaries. The sooner you establish boundaries at the early stages of growing up , the earlier the child relinquishes such habits, hence the second primary reason for setting boundaries with kids is to stop bad behaviors early. You need to let your kids know at their early development stages that they are not supposed to accept any gift from strangers.

It is important for parents to understand that kids do not understand the issue of power struggle; hence parents must make their children understand who is in charge. Children that are not raised with consistent and firm authority may likely end up with low self-esteem, but you must not exercise extreme authority on them because they may psychologically feel inadequate to handle things by themselves. Never tell your child "Oh please don't hurt me", rather, you must tell him "Don't hit me, hitting hurts people". Being affirmative with actions or boundaries will send clear authority and signal to your children.

Parents will need to learn and adapt to physical boundaries themselves, this will ensure that they do not go too hard on their children when they go out of control. Inflicting injuries on kids are not the best possible way of setting limits or making affirmative statements, rather, they will be afraid of confiding in you or communicating certain information to you. When you set limit with your children in the hard way, such kids will learn destructive behaviors and start damaging other people's properties or inflicting their friends or mates with injuries and that could lead to legal issues. It is important for parents to set limits at the early stages in order to deal with bad behaviors in their children in the safest possible way.

The most angelic baby today may learn the act of aggression quickly, and children often show aggressive behaviors when they are also sick and tired of certain situations, and for this reasons, parents must learn the consequences of setting certain boundaries as well as the punishment for the violation of such boundaries. Boundaries set with kids are different from those set for marriages, kids are still young and naïve, hence certain boundaries may be too harsh for them, you need to understand the mental and physical abilities of your children before setting boundaries with them.

Chapter 26
Before you set boundaries with your children

Children will generally want to know where they stand and what rules you want to enforce. As your children learn to work their ways through growth and development, one of your primary roles is to provide boundaries and guidelines to see that they do not fall into troubles. Some boundaries don't have to be set, they already existed and most of them are physical boundaries- for instance the pavements and road user signs are boundaries your kids must know to avoid physical injuries.

When adequate boundaries are put in place, you will easily provide a framework to keep your kids safe and adequately supported. Boundaries will provide guidelines for your children's behavior, and will also help them understand the behaviors that are socially acceptable. Boundaries are designed to help children learn self-discipline and with time, they will learn to set boundaries for themselves.

By setting boundaries you will help a child understand the acceptable code of behavior. Just before you set the boundaries, you need to note that boundary setting is easier said than done,

We all know that it is not proper to punish a baby, but the best way of setting boundaries for them is to distract them away from a situation that makes them act in certain annoying ways. Even the toddlers and matured kids will need some soft handling occasionally, even though punishing them will help them understand certain limitations to their freedom. As a baby reaches his 10th month he realizes that he can make certain impacts on his environment, and this is healthy for his growth and development, however, you need to start setting boundaries for her at this point as he realizes his own power to do certain things- for instance changing the TV channel while you are watching your favorite TV program, if you allow him to change the TV as often as he likes, he can become addicted to the habit , and if he does this , you must not get angry or scold him, you need to simply say No and take him away from the TV remote control.

You may not be able to force infants and babies less than 12 months from violating certain boundaries, but you can successfully distract them. Staying consistent with boundaries but not becoming overly reactive is the best possible way to set boundaries for babies.

Setting discipline begins when a baby attain his or her first year of birth. If you baby goes hungry, you must feed him, if his diaper is wet, you must change it, and if he cries, you must attend to him, but babies grow wiser quickly and his needs may certain become wants – this is when you should introduce the boundaries.

Discipline is not about punishment; rather it is about teaching and guiding your children through boundary setting. For this reason the best time to start setting boundaries are when the babies begin to get smarter.

You need to understand that setting limits are part of your duties as a parent, because limits help your child understand the differences between right and wrong. While some babies that misbehave may not be doing so intentionally, for instance , when he is tugging at your glasses, he is not intentionally doing that but trying to explore the world around him. You need to understand that your baby will always observe things around him and he will want to stay connected to anything that catches his fancy- he may start dropping items off the chair to see how they break or splashes – this is the period you should start setting the boundaries and you may introduce slight punishment for him to stop such habits.

Children needs to understand what is expected of them to behave in the most appropriate manner, however, this does not mean you should give them too many rules that can become too complicated and too confusing. Not giving them too much rules or boundaries but giving them basic rules will help them understand the values of having such rules and these can motivate them in cooperating with you at the long run. Simple rules such as having a decent conversation with them instead of shouting with one another, or asking them to learn how to take permission to borrow things instead of taking such things at their own will can help set boundaries for them.

Stating rules as regarding children in a positive manner, instead of telling them all the time about what to do, works best .when you set limits for children, you must give them clear directions as to what you are expecting from them. Letting them know what to expect from them will also serve as a basis or guide in similar situations, hence you don't have to repeat your instructions or set multiple boundaries around similar situations.

Chapter 27
Types of boundaries to set for kids

There are quite a number of boundaries you can set around your kids and these boundaries serve different purposes at different times. There are basically three types of boundaries you can set for your kids, these are;

- Protection from Physical harms or injuries,

- Communicating with the rest of the family

- Looking after people or things, and

- Showing respect to others

Setting the Limits

Type of Limit	boundaries	Affirmative actions
Protection against physical harm	Don't go outside the door Stop poking at your brother	Stay within the yard, the street is busy with too many cars and you might get knocked down. Be gentle with your kid brother, he is too small for such rough play

Taking care of things	Don't leave your toys lying around the living room Stop doing that!	Pack up your toys right now and keep them in the shelve before you go to bed. Take your ball outside if you want to play, something might get broken if you play it inside.
Showing care and respect to others	Stop being mean to our visitor Don't take your sister's toys	You must play in a friendly way and make sure Peter has a turn too. Ask your sister first before you borrow her toys. You would want her to ask you before taking your toys.

Communicating with the rest of the family	You must always greet everyone when you wake up in the morning.	I wouldn't answer you if you shout at me again!
Don't yell at me	Never shout angrily at me when you need something	

Following Up on Boundaries

You need to ensure that you provide positive consequences for every positive reaction to boundaries – this will encourage your children to comply with such rules and expectations, for instance, when children do what you asked them to do, try as much as possible to praise or thank them. Secondly , you must expect some lapses when your children are trying to adjust to new behaviors or boundaries , for instance, you may have to remind your kids about the consequences of nagging or shouting at you frequently.

You should learn to create some checklists or reward charts, these will help you keep track of positive behaviors and also ensure that they get motivated to complete assigned tasks. In a situation where children repeatedly ignore your reasonable and clear instructions, you may have to apply some logical consequences, these are directed at stopping the undesired activities rather than punishing your children unnecessarily-for instance ;

You can withdraw the child from the situation especially when the situation will likely end up being destructive or harmful. Withdrawal of privileges can also be used as a form of punishment especially when an item such as toy is being misused or neglected. You can withdraw a toy that is being fought over or used in an unsafe manner by your kids.

Chapter 28
How to set Healthy boundaries for your children

The purpose of setting boundaries with your children is to protect them without being harsh. Some boundaries may require that you become tricky when setting boundaries, most especially when you are trying to avoid issues such as threats. You may also apply the Calm and firm boundary approach especially when your parenting muscles need to be exercise fully.

When your child has just behaved so rude and or unsafe, your emotions will naturally run high, and you may be sent into either a fight or flight mood. When you allow the downside of your emotions to take complete control of you, your ability of thinking positively decreases. You cannot set healthy boundaries for your children when your emotions are unregulated. Here are some of the tips for parents in creating boundaries with your kids;

Tip 1: Try as much as possible to think ahead

You need to be strategic when planning boundaries with your kids, and this simply means you must be a step ahead of your kids. As adults, our brains are more complex and more developed than the brains of young ones, and we also understand places where our kids can make mistake and injure themselves but most babies are not aware of this, hence your planning must be centered around areas where your kids and weak to control. You need to take your space and think things thoroughly before setting boundaries. You need to understand where your limits lie ahead of the season.

Tip 2: Wishy washy languages will not help in setting boundaries

You may have to record yourself and play the recordings back while planning your boundaries. You will likely hear some verbal habits that must be removed when you hear yourself. You will also hear several weak languages especially when you are trying to give directives while setting your limits. Never use statements such as "I really don't want you to do that", in your boundaries, however you must be affirmative and always stand your ground with a commanding tone when you set boundaries.

Tip 3: Always check your facial expression and body language when you set boundaries

Non-verbal cues are as important as verbal boundary setting with children, and you don't have to go all day singing and shouting about your boundaries to children because you already appear big to them. Your facial expression, and body language should communicate enough information to your children when they are getting out of boundary.

Tip 4: Make sure you produce a warm but firm tone

A very sharp tone of voice can be very scary to little babies, and such tone can set up an instant fight or fright alarm in their mind, likewise yelling at babies will also create some fear in them, hence you must save such tones for emergencies only. A scared baby will only comply with your boundaries only when you successfully disconnect him from you, and such a child may not have emotional feelings for you again, however a warm but firm tone, will keep the child within boundaries without creating fear in his mind.

Tip 5: Never expect a child to comply with new boundaries without feeling upset

You need to set limits where necessary but you must also leave some spaces for feelings. It is often unrealistic to expect a No from you in everything, but he will accept No from you always if you are calm and reassuring. The tough feelings of not getting what a child wants can make him become emotionally heated, but such heated arguments will disappear when boundaries are set with a calm and reassuring way. Do not attempt to shut down your children because you want them to stay within boundaries, such shut down will make them emotionally upset.

Tip 6: Have realistic and developmental expectations

The best possible way to evaluate the successes of the boundaries set by you is to expect some developmental expectations from your children. For most kids within ages of 10 months and 3 years, they always want to get into everything, and wouldn't share their stuffs without some protests, while 4 year old's always want to know why you did certain things. 5 year old's can become sassy and older kids can become very stubborn. The key to setting boundaries successfully is to brush up the key areas where your child has developed higher intelligence. You need to understand that kids grow emotionally, physically and psychologically at each level. You should have different expectation on your kid at different developmental levels.

Tip 7: Remain decisive even when you change your mind

You need to remain confident in your decisions if you want your kids to comply with boundaries successfully. It is either you stop your babies from jumping on the bed when you want to sleep than giving them specific days when they can indulge in such acts. Staying consistent with the rules is more important that setting punishments when they break rules.

Tip 8: Be physical with the boundaries only when necessary

Many parents believe that the only way to enforce boundaries is to get physical with children when the reverse is actually the case. Do not get physical with enforcing boundaries unless you become frustrated with a child's deliberate negative attitudes. You need to pay close attention to be sure that you are not hurting them, sometimes a brief moment of contact is needed and you should withdraw once the child is able to control himself safely.

Tip 9: Add some humor to the boundaries being set

Kids love to be entertained sometime, and entertainments work much faster and better than other ways of boundary settings. Make use of some silly voice tone or a funny character to explain the reason behind the boundaries and your babies will learn to obey you. Listen to the feelings of babies, if you want them to stay connected to you. Try as much as possible to dress like their famous comic heroes to explain the dangers in doing certain negative things.

Step by step approach to setting healthy boundaries with children

Step 1: Invite quality time in building a steady relationship with your children

You don't just wakeup someday and decide to set boundaries with your children, you need to develop a healthy relationship with them first, and that is when you can explain new rules and limits to them before they eventually see such rules.

Step 2: Try as much as possible to do some homework

You need to have some reflection, especially on boundaries set by other parents and see how such boundaries have worked. With good homework done, you will be able to establish clear boundaries with others. You can do some research on boundaries by engaging in the following steps;

- Make a clarification on what you want to teach your children, for instance to develop a healthy sense of self hygiene.

- Examine your parenting style, have a consideration for things you can tweak in, in order for your children to learn what exactly you want them to learn.

- what are you own personal boundaries? Consider how your personal boundaries can be incorporated with your children's boundaries.

Step3: Start by establishing basic boundaries or limits

There are some rules that can serve as basis for setting boundaries with your children, these include the following;

- I possess the right to say No to people when they influence my kids negatively, and without feeling guilty for saying no.

- I will never tolerate any abuse on my children for any reason.

- I have the right to personal privacy, even from my kids.

- My kids have the right to express their dissatisfaction

Boundaries must be set in a clear, respectful and reciprocal relationships for kids, and you must be mindful of the fact that your children's boundaries must be respected. Make sure that all boundaries are stated in simple and clear terms, and you must also provide some brief reasons for the limits or boundaries. Make sure you introduce a pause in-between each limit to allow the kids digest each of them.

Step 4: Try as much as possible to involve other children and young individuals

One of the best possible ways of modeling your boundaries is to engage other kids as well as younger adults in setting boundaries with children. You need to engage the co-operation of other people because it creates some sense of fairness in your own kids, and they get to know that you are not intentionally punishing them, but ensuring that they are well protected.

Step 5: Deal effectively with the violation of boundaries

Positive boundary guidance techniques are needed to be put in place to ensure that kids don't violate boundaries frequently, similarly , soft punishment should be deployed to guide children about consequences of violating boundaries, however, punishments for boundary violation should vary depending on the ages of the kids. You need to negotiate with your kids on the consequences they will face when a boundary is not respected. In order to maintain some sense of fairness, you must ensure that consequences are in tune with or related to the boundaries being violated- for instance, if a child continues to mess his room up by misplacing his toys, then the consequence should be to clean up after him before dinner is served.

Children will have to be reminded of their limits, as well as the reasons for such limits and the consequences for breaking them.

Step 6: Get some support

If you are setting boundaries for the first time as a parent, it will be important to get some help. Maintaining certain boundaries with others will become simpler when we get help from other parents, psychologists, and even on the internet. You need to consider what exactly will be supportive enough, it could be a brief conversation with a friend at the gym about how he or she was able to set boundaries effectively for his or her own children, or having discussions with a professional on ways to deal with uncooperative children.

Chapter 29
Common problems with setting boundaries with children

There are quite a number of problems associated with setting boundaries with children and these problems could be caused by parents and children. The commonest problems with setting boundaries with kids are;

- Non acceptance of boundaries,

- Lack of proper communication,

- Improper boundaries, and

- Irresponsiveness

Non-acceptance of boundaries

Generally speaking, no kid wants to be limited; hence it can be very difficult for kids to accept changes especially when such new boundaries are abrupt without any prior notice. It is important for parents to enforce boundaries gradually and not abruptly, doing this will help the child learn to cope or adjust to the new boundaries.

Lack of Proper communication

Lack of proper communication may lead to chaos in enforcing new boundaries. When you do not engage in proper research, you wouldn't understand the needs and challenges of your children and you may end up introducing wrong boundaries. You need to communicate your concerns and feelings with your children and learn to read meanings to their feelings so that you don't give them extreme boundaries that may cause more harm than good to their physical and mental health.

Setting improper boundaries

You need to learn to set boundaries appropriate for the age of each kid, otherwise you may set boundaries that are either too lenient or too harsh. Kids less than 10 months of age cannot deal with any kind of limit, however, children older than 12 months should have behavioral and protective boundaries because they are matured enough to start understanding the difference between good and bad. The older your children gets, the bigger or more severe the punishments they should face for violating boundaries. Aside from age, other factors that should be considered when setting proper boundaries for children include; gender, mental ability, and health conditions. Try as much as possible to avoid setting boundaries that can put your kids in difficult situations.

Irresponsiveness

Irresponsiveness to certain boundaries could be a deliberate act from kids who simply don't like the boundaries you set. While some kids may withdraw from their parents, others will deliberately break such boundaries just to show their displeasures. While some parents become aggressive with irresponsive kids, others will simply remove such boundaries and allow their children to continue indulging in certain habits. The best possible way to deal with an irresponsive child to new boundaries is to educate the child about the dangers in his behavior and if he remains irresponsive then you need to introduce consequences that will force him or her respect the boundaries. Experts believe that foods and affection should not be used as punishment for irresponsive children.

Chapter 30:
The Origins of Mind Control

Earliest Record of Mind Control

Mind control has been around for decades though it is important to understand its earliest origins so as to discern how it is relevant today. Trephining is the earliest historical practice that reveals evidence of techniques for mind control. This involved cutting a hole in the skill of an individual who is thought to be possessed by evil spirits. It is expected that the evil spirits would exit the body through this hole. This was perhaps the first known treatment for mental illness, with the intention of altering behaviors which were social unacceptable.

The next example of mind control techniques is perhaps exorcism. People who were being exorcised may have had an early equivalent of psychological illness such as multiple personality disorder which is also known as a dissociative disorder. The method used involved holding a person down and praying, yelling and splashing holy water until the behavior changed signifying the release of a demon.

Systemizing Mind Control

Forward a century or so, and the next example of mind control comes from a textbook called the Malleus Maleficarum that was written in 1484. It has often been referred to as the Witch's Hammer. The Malleus Maleficarum outlined a "systemization of the knowledge of how to do interrogations to lead people to give confessions that you want them to give." This was a way of controlling people to get a particular result, whether or not the person liked it. Inquisitors in the middle ages used this work to get all sorts of confessions, whether they were real or false.

By the 1800'as, the Malleus Maleficarum was being adopted by police departments as the early development of the police manual. This was also at the birth of psychiatry. At the time, psychiatric treatments had elements of violence, just like the ones used to cast out demons during exorcisms.

Mind Control and Psychiatry

What happened is that psychiatric treatments included elements of restraint and violence. Patients believed to have mental illness, demon possession or be of unsound mind, were exposed to a range of treatments to 'get them to be of sound mind'. These techniques included restraint with a straightjacket, where a person would be tied to a pipe in a wall.

By the 1900's, mind control techniques evolved to include shock treatment. As electricity was still in its early days and not available everywhere, water shock treatment was the treatment of choice. This was often done by placing the person blindfolded on a platform and then having them suddenly fall into a bucket of ice cold water. This technique was used to get people to tell 'the truth' especially if it had been thought that they were lying.

If someone was suspected of being possessed, especially if they said things that others did not agree with, there were other shock treatments introduced. These were alternative forms of mind control. Noise shock treatment was one, and it involved firing a canon being fired from behind a person without them, being aware that this was about to happen. This was meant to be a violent cure for the possession.

By looking at this history, it becomes evident that mind control began with the study of the human mind as well as mental illness from a theory around possession and curing based on violence.

Next, psychiatrists determined that to understand what is happening in the brain, you need to know what is happening outside the brain.

The Advent of Hypnosis

Mind control techniques became more acute with the introduction of hypnosis. Hypnosis relies heavily on the laws of suggestion as a method to control the mind. Mesmer, who developed theories of hypnosis, used the technique to 'cure' people of their mental afflictions. At the time, it was considered that all this was a result of the power of imagination, thought it would be decades later that a link between manipulation and creativity would be established.

It was also believed that hypnosis could control of person's mind and push them into a state o hypnotic seduction whereby they would be an inevitable attraction between the hypnotist and the hypnotized. Hypnosis was used as a form of entertainment, mind control to get people to do things out of the ordinary, such as drinking milk from a saucer on the floor.

From hypnosis, there was a belief that thosehypnotized would have 'false memory symptoms'. This would have them saying the wrong things in a hypnotized state while sincerely believing they were right. This was dangerous, particularly in the court of law.

New Mind Control Techniques in Practice

A.R.Lucia in the 1920's was looking for other members of mind control, to do more than just get people to report n events that had not occurred. He also intended to get the people to actually experience a whole range of emotions which were affiliated to such events.

The success of this mind control technique is evidenced in the Moscow Show Trials, where Stalin put his former friends on trial, and they confessed to a range of crimes which they did not commit, and they also begged to be executed as enemies of the state.

Following this, intelligence agencies in the United States of America began to notice the potential of mind control techniques. At this juncture, Edward Hunter in the 1940's coined the term known as brainwashing, which looks at controlling the mind with a combination of hypnosis and drugs.

Mind Control and Sensory Deprivation

The next step to mind control was sensory deprivation. This involved putting people in a trance like state so that they could decrease the sensory input to the mind. People would then have a hallucination and believe in those hallucinations. They were usually kept in isolation although if they were isolated for too long, they would become psychotic.

Solomon Ashe then studied mind control caused by social pressure. He would select a class and bribe all but one person. He would then draw two lines, one long and one short. When asking the class which was the long line, all would refer to the short one except the person being bribed. After a short while, the person who had not been bribed would conform and agree so that they can fit in the group.

This was evidence that manipulation did not necessarily require physical coercion. The focus shifted to social influences and how people were unaware that they were being manipulated. Next, mind control was studied in its relation to obeying authority figures. Milgram found that it was easy to manipulate people with the simplest commands as they would not object to authority figures.

Today, mind control picks elements from all the historical forms used, even the most primitive ones. Read on to discover how mind control has been applied, using manipulation, persuasion and deception.

Chapter 31:
Understanding Mind Control

Taking control of other people's mind is possible. It is not a new thing at all, and it is not entirely a good thing but when used for the right purposes, it can help not only you but a large population. Mind control is not about making the other person a mindless zombie but about influencing them in the right way. Depending on the need at hand, it can be of great help to the people involved and to the society in general.

Mind control is mainly used by the people who study behavior in order to convince a vast mass of people to follow the will of a smaller group. It seems a hard task to achieve but an expert in this can do it successfully. Marketers do it all the time in order to get to sell an individual product. They take the time to study the target group so as to market to them something they are sure will be of help to the people. This is a good way to use mind control.

Today, mind control is used for different reasons by different people. It is used psychologically as well as technologically. The good thing is that the effects of mind control can be reduced or eliminated altogether after the said purpose has been achieved, which is great news. Mind control is however not allowed in case it is going to bring harm to the person being controlled.

Mind control is a fascinating subject for many people, the thought of being able to control the minds of others, getting them to do what you want give the illusion of power. It has been discussed in many contexts, and can be referred to using various names. These names include brainwashing, uninformed consent, manipulation, deception, exploitive and coercive persuasion. An example of people who are believed to be experiencing mind control are those who are members of religious or other cults.

It is clear that discussing mind control is likely to bring forth loaded reactions from certain people. These reactions are often based on fear from their pre-conceived ideas, rather than from the mind control itself. To understand the essence of mind control, you should clear your mind and dismiss the thoughts of all stereotypes.

Mind control is rooted in human psychology, particularly in understanding how it can affect a person's behavior and thinking. Although it is often portrayed as something inherently negative, it does not have to be. It is possible to practice mind control without excessively using deception or using coercive persuasion.

Positive Mind Control

One could say that mind control is applied to most modern methods of advertising. Take, for example, the typical television advert for a product. There is often one end goal for the advert, and that is a call to action from the customer. That convincing message may be considered as a form of coercive persuasion.

What happens is the marketers need to figure out a way that they can get hold of your attention and ensure that you keep paying attention to the message. Through music, movement and words, the marketer is able to use the television advert to get you into a trance like state. You are able to remain in this state for the length of the advert due to persuasive images being used.

Some of the most persuasive images include baby animals, human babies and anything with sexual connotations. By using these images, they try to gently persuade you to buy a product, and this is a very basic form of mind control.

Positive mind control can be used to improve every aspect of life. This involves teaching techniques that promote positive thinking consistently until the mind stops delving into negative thoughts. To get a positive space with mind control, you can teach yourself how to shift your thoughts through exercises, visualizing and using electronic frequencies to achieve mind control.

Positive mind control dies not involve controlling others and forcing them to behave in certain ways. It is more about learning how to control your mind so that you can live positively.

Negative Mind Control

There is a dark side to mind control, and it involves arousing negative emotions in the intended subject. These negative emotions include guilt, shame or fear. These are the types of emotions that you will find in the members of many groups, as this is a good way to control their minds as well as keep them in line and stop them from leaving.

When this type of mind control is being used, the intention is usually to completely strip the members of the core of their personality so that it is easier for them to conform to the group. This is accomplished by using deception, lies and the control of information.

The reason people get so easily sucked into mind control situations or groups is the fact that they have only limited information about the group. Therefore, their decisions are made at surface value. Once interactions continue and, involvement deepens, especially if the financial investment or time has been used, it becomes very challenging to leave. The existing members have often resigned themselves to being stuck in the situation.

These give an idea of what positive and negative mind control entail. However, anyone who is being suppressed or manipulated can be said to be under some form of mind control. This includes people in abusive marriages and dysfunctional families when there could be a lot of negative mind control.

Know when you need protection from Mind Control

Here are some scenarios that people believe to be mind control situations.

1) The influence parents have over their children in moral, social and personal standards.

2) Modifying your behaviour through self-discipline.

3) Drugging a person so that you can take advantage of them.

4) Dehumanizing prisoners so that they become more compliant.

5) Aggressively delivering religious messages.

6) Listening to certain self-help tapes.

When deciding what constitutes mind control and what does not, you need to remember one thing; mind control involves a person being unable to freely choose their behavior. If you find that you can control your own thoughts through self-discipline, then it is unlikely that you have fallen victim to mind control.

Mind control exists in a semi-permanent state. Therefore, if the state of mind can quickly be altered because of a simple variable, then the mind is not under anyone's control. Mind control requires actual control of another person, rather than having the other person in a controllable position. Therefore, people who are under the influence of drugs and alcohol cannot qualify as being mind-controlled.

The reason that it is so easy to get caught off guard with mind control is due to the people who are likely to use it. They could include good friends and people, they could be just like you, and they could need to change their behavior so that they can be in the right frame of mind.

How does mind control work?

In order to understand how mind control can work so powerfully in a person's life, it is imperative to break it down its different actions. Mind control requires coercion, which involves restraining by force. Some people think of mind control as something that you do to drive one crazy. This would require physical restraining and threatening behavior to get a person to conform to a particular ideology.

In addition, there is an element of persuasion in mind control, where a person is impaired or compelled to do something through a step by step application of psychological pressure. Once coercion and persuasion are put together in particular settings, the result is a manipulation of the mind to subdue certain behaviors and to bring forth other ones. Changing the way someone thinks and what they believe in can be a more effective method of mind control than any physical force or torture.

Older concepts on mind control entailed a significant amount of physical torture and drug use to get a person to conform to a certain way of behavior. This was often backed up with aggressive threats which made people do things that were against their will. The reason that this does not count as mind control is that the overall attitude has not changed. Given a chance to escape, the person will revert back to their normal way of being.

Coercive persuasion is much more effective as a method of mind control because you can actually change a person's attitude and behavior without their knowledge or permission. With this method, the subject develops a willingness to do things that they have never done before, and this is a complete change of both their natural behavior and their attitude.

Chapter 32:
Mind Control and Human Psychology

Once you have understood the history of mind control, it becomes easier to place and understand where it fits in with human psychology. In a sense, mind control is all about human psychology, specifically focusing on the brain and how one can affect the behavior of another person. It is about getting people to react to subtle messages, even if they ordinarily would not. It entails doing this without the person's knowledge.

It is believed that for most humans, they begin to feel the effects of mind control from the time that they enter kindergarten and go through their early years of schooling. They go through a process that is known as psychological conditioning, which is a method used to prepare children's young minds to accept a particular type of programming. This programming is usually in direct contrast to the children themselves, and of most of the people on earth.

Take, for example, an education system that encourages memorization instead of practical learning. It is common knowledge that people learn from their mistakes. That once you fail at something, you try again until you get it right. However, there are education systems that do not support this thinking. Instead, they teach children to memorize information, rather than learn. The focus becomes how much you can remember, rather than what you can apply. The result is a nation full of people who are not empowered to take action, but are filled with propaganda and unhelpful information.

With this sort of base, it becomes easier to see how many other forms of psychological control can be placed on adults. There are many places in the world where the adults are living with a twisted form of reasoning as their primary reference point.

Once one completes their education and goes out into the real world, mind control continues through mass media. Human beings are conditioned in regards to what they believe and what they want. An example of this is the introduction of religion around the world. When missionaries travelled to faraway lands to preach their gospel, they managed to convince the people in the places that they landed that their method of prayer and worship was superior to what was in practice in the area. Even though people may not have fully understood what that meant, they were manipulated with words into changing their beliefs.

Psychology and Sociology

Psychology and Sociology have provided an excellent platform for the study of mind control. The first studies (and some other studies to this day) were conducted on animals, and their reactions used as the basis of an application to human beings. The initial experiments looked at how animals responded to stimuli.

It was found that creating an association between a sound and food will lead to repeat behaviour amongst does. Once they hear the sound associated with food, even if they cannot smell the food they will go towards where they typically retrieve the food. This is all an aspect of psychological conditioning.

In essence, this reviews the reactions to certain triggers, and how triggers can determine behavior. If there are similar triggers in human beings, people can be controlled to do a range of different things. This is what the mass media communication counts on. By creating associations and triggers in the messages that they send out, they can influence the behavior of the watchers or customers.

To take it a step further, the mind is conditioned towards viewing a trigger in a three-pronged solution. This can be referred to as identifying the problem, then generating a reaction and finally choosing to follow a pre-planned solution. What happens, especially when people are concerned for their safety and that of their loved ones, they behave in ways that are out of character.

Suddenly, a person will beg for mercy or for a threat or problem to be removed. They idea is to get back to a place of peace and understanding. Manipulation of this sort has resulted in people reluctantly going to fight in wars.

Psychological Conditioning

Today, psychological conditioning as a method of mind control is often used by retailers or businesses looking to get people to consume their products or services. The message that is often sent out is that once one experiences their merchandise, then they will be happy. The message is that shopping will make you feel good and solve your problems.

The long-term effect of this type of conditioning is that people now believe that in order to enjoy happiness, they need to buy things and elevate their social status. Until they are able to do this, they will go through periods where they are extremely unhappy.

Further psychological conditioning has been studied to understand what effects there were on mind control. A study in 1965 looking at tortured dogs wanted to ascertain whether dogs would escape when punished. The results revealed that once the dogs realized that there was no way out, they actually stopped trying to get away and escape.

This type of conditioning is very evident in the world we are living in today. When a person feels as though their civil liberties are not being allowed, or a change was promised and things are still the same, we choose to give up. Giving up is easier than taking a stand and facing consequences.

There are a range of psychological techniques that can be used to prove mind control. These include observing people who are facing peer pressure, are willing to obey and will conform to authority. You can work towards getting this group of people to do something that they normally would not do.

In addition to psychological conditioning, human psychology also examines how people influence each other, and that has to do with persuasion. Persuasion is a tool that many people use when they are trying to control another person, or to get them to think along my wavelength.

There are certain ways that have been revealed in relation to a person's ability to be an influencer. These are: -

a) Understanding a person's motivations so that you can determine the best way to influence them

b) Speak passionately using swear words if you have to as people can then emotionally connect with your point of view.

c) Use your voice and be the loudest. Always give your opinion. In the end, it will be believed that your opinion adequately represents the entire group.

d) When asking a person for something, speak to then in the right ear. They are likely to comply with the request, even if it something that they would not ordinarily do.

Human Psychology and Manipulation

Human psychology and its understanding has greatly benefited many people. Using techniques like mindfulness can help improve behavior and understanding different mindsets. However, psychology still has a dark side – one that is exploited through manipulation.

According to human psychology, a person's actions has two causes. These are "Nature" and "Nurture". Nature looks at what is within us as human beings and includes our instincts and emotions. Nurture is everything that is learned in a person's surroundings.

Think about the messages you would see in marketing. A car sales person may place an attractive lady in their showroom to appeal to the desires of men. This is a simple way of manipulating the natural instincts of a man to get him to purchase the car.

People also are inclined to want to think well of themselves. They can be manipulated intochanging their thinking through underhand tactics. These affect a person at a subconscious level psychologically, which in turn leads to a lack of confidence and a change in behavior.

It is possible to be manipulated through hearing hurtful words, being dismissed in conversations, experiencing a person undermine you, and even continuous shouting.

People who are being manipulated begin to doubt themselves and their abilities. These tactics are often used to meet an agenda.

Understanding Aggression

Manipulation in human psychology also involves understanding aggression. It should be possible to be able to conceal aggressive behaviors and intentions. This requires you to be aware of your opponent's personality and thinking, so that you can identify any psychological vulnerability they may have and then craft psychological weapons that you can use against them.

This type of aggression is covert and often done is such a veiled way that it cannot be detected. This is because someone who is manipulating you does not want you to resist, yet they are intent on achieving their goals. Manipulation is effective because psychologically, you may believe that you are getting the most of you.

In psychology, manipulation is difficult to notice at a conscious level. However, within your subconscious, you will realize that there is something wrong and that you have been pushed too far. You are likely to be quite defensive. Due to what is appearing at the conscious level, you are unlikely to notice you're being manipulated.

A person who is skilled at manipulation will prey on people who are very sensitive and conscientious. They can manipulate through playing the victim or finding ways to shame. This works on these kind of people because they are uncomfortable with seeing others miserable, and they do not want to feel negative about themselves and rational when it came to others, and their circumstances are usually avoided by manipulators, as their tactics would not give the right result.

Human Psychology and Persuasion

Try and imagine a day where there was no persuasion. Where no one asks you what you are doing, or what you can buy to make your life better. If you take a moment and think about it, you will realize that it is virtually impossible to spend a day away from persuasion.

People see most of their persuasive messages on the media. So how do they react to these messages? This comes down to imagery, particularly what people see as they take in these messages. Over time, marketers have been able to deposit subliminal messages into the psych of customers who make purchases.

These subliminal messages encourage people to buy particular brands, certain quantities and even foods which are bundled together. For example, when in the shop, every time that you purchase cereal you will automatically also buy milk.

There are many different types of persuasion techniques that can be adopted. The primary goal of using persuasion should be to convince someone of your argument and have them adopt a new attitude based on you so that it can shape their core beliefs.

Tips on Using Persuasion

To get to someone psychologically using persuasion, a person can: -

1) Create a need which a person believes is fundamental. Take, for example, the need for perfume. Even though this is not a requirement for survival, some people will be physically uncomfortable when they cannot get access to perfume.

2) Consider their social needs because every person wants to be popular, or similar to those that are around then. This type of persuasion can be seen in the media, where people are encouraged to purchase different items so that they can fit in with the crowd.

3) When communicating, loaded words will do the trick because you can convince someone that an imperfection is a perfection by applying the right grammar to the situation. Therefore describing food as low fat or high fiber, you are more likely to get a response and a result.

An example of the effect of persuasion on human psychology is as follows. When a waiter delivers a customer's bill, he expects his normal to at 14%, however, because the waiter did something that was nice and appreciated, the customer gave an even larger tip. This is because when someone does something nice for you, it become very easy to pay them back.

Restaurants also create a sense of urgency that affects a person waiting for a meal. They do this by not including every member of the family if they need to deal with an emergency.

One of the oldest persuasion techniques is amplifying the kettle.

All in all, persuasion is highly relevant as an element that is used for mind control. If you want to be more persuasive, you can try to speak a person's language, which means that you understand how they communicate, and communicate with them.

Human Psychology and Deception

Human beings are known to be liars, no matter where they are from and no matter what he situation may be. Deception is in effect lying, and it is a typical human behavior. The consequences of lying are immense, they could affect a person socially, financially and personally. They could lead to mistrust or broken relationships.

However, when considering mind control, lying is taken to the next level, where it is referred to as deception. When you deceive someone, you deliberately set out to give them the wrong information so that they are unable to deal with or handle a particular situation. There are a range of reasons that people would be deceptive, including fear, self-preservation and trying to fit in. All these are valid, somewhat harmless reasons.

With mind control, the deception goes so much deeper. In this case, it refers to how a person deceives themselves so that they can believe an ideology that is foreign to their consciousness.

This type of deception can be initiated by another person through one effective technique, and that is repetition. People who are in abusive marriages often find that their belief systems has changed because of the mind control techniques used by their violent spouse. A beautiful woman could be repeatedly told how unattractive and unappealing she is, and even though she knows it now to be true, over time, she begins to internalize this method and then she loses all confidence and believes it.

In fact, she will believe it so deeply that it would be difficult to get her back to her original mindset. That is the power that deception has on a person.

There are people who use self-deception as a way to control other people. Take, for example, a political figure who has been caught in a lie. Rather than admit to it, he begins to deny its possibility, even if there is irrefutable evidence. He shares information that hints at a conspiracy, where everyone is out to get him. The more he denies it, the easier it is to divide people into two camps, those who believe him and those who don't.

The mind control is basically in those who believe him. More often than not they will have a cult following for the political figure where he can do no wrong. In addition, they will fully support anything that the figure says or does. This is an example of people getting sucked in by deception.

Chapter 33:
Mind Control and Manipulation

Each and every person on the planet has experienced some form of manipulation. This goes without question. If at this point you are shaking your head and your mind is telling you it has never happened to you, this chapter will explain to you how it has.

When picturing manipulation, many people will consider or believe that it happens to a person who is weak, unable to stand up for themselves, naïve or maybe even a victim of abuse. While these types of people may be at higher risk of experiencing manipulation even a well-educated, confident and self-assured individual can be manipulated.

The reason that manipulation works so well as a mind control tactic lies in its subtlety. Over a period of time, you can subtly experience methods of manipulation, and the way it works, you are unlikely to ever know that you had been manipulated.

Mind Control and Manipulation under Pressure

Most people have an idea of how they would react when placed under pressure. They would be confident, they would take action, and they would do what is necessary to resolve the situation. Others will take the high road, be the hero or maintain calm. The truth is until a person is in this situation; they have no idea how they would react. If you are under attack by violent robbers, would you still behave as you normally do? What if your family is under attack too, by someone you know and respect? How would you react then? In instances like this, there is no telling how one would react to pressure. When under immense pressure, we open ourselves up to manipulation.

Here is an example of manipulation in modern literature, Lord of the Flies, is a book by William Golding, where a group of boys find themselves stranded on an island. One of the boys, Jack, manages to manipulate some of the other boys, to the extent that they were willing to resort to murder in order to survive.

He is able to do this by playing on their emotions. The situation that they were in had them experiencing two main emotions – fear and excitement. He started his manipulation by getting the boys adrenaline pumping, putting them in a state of primal excitement when hunting a pig. After he caught the pig, and while the boys were still pumped up, he suggested that one of them be hunted as a pig. Now addicted to the feeling of excitement, the other bots blindly follow Jack.

When Jack notices that the adrenaline rush is waning, he adds to the manipulation by incorporating fear. He spoke to them about a beast that might attack and insisted that for their safety, they would need to spend less time around a fire and more time hunting. As the boys become hysterical, Jack realizes he is in control just as he planned to be.

This example illustrates a group mentality and general behaviors can change during times of stress. The boys are having had little to no exposure to hunting before, enjoyed the experience and the 'rush' that it provided. Most of the boys chose to conform rather than stick up for themselves. This is a form of manipulation through mind control, and it is known as groupthink. Deindividuation also occurred here, and it refers to people behaving out of character when they are in a crowd.

When a person of authority is in control, rather than object to anything, people will change their opinions to fit in with the authority figure's desire. How this becomes mind control and not just basic manipulation is that after all is complete, people are likely to rationally explain their behavior, and they will convince themselves that they actively made the decision to act the way they did. There would be a vehement denial of manipulation on their part.

Mind Control and Manipulation through Priming

Priming involves a change in a person's behavior without any conscious awareness on their part. A simple example, consider the following sentence, 'it was snowy and freezing cold, and the people were shaking.' You are likely to have rubbed your arms at the end of this sentence and given a little shiver, even if you are in a warm climate. You had been primed for cold weather. This is something subtle but highly effective.

People have been using priming techniques for years to influence behavior. Priming is a method of dominating as well as manipulating other people in order to achieve their own ends. Supermarkets use a layout that primes people towards spending. Fast moving consumer products like juices or snacks are usually located far away from the entrance. In order to purchase them, a buyer needs to walk through scores of products to reach them. In that process, they are likely to buy something that was not on their planned list.

You can be sure people have been primed if they adopt violent behavior to support their beliefs. This is usually done through social conditioning.

Mind Control, Manipulation and the Government

Conspiracy theorists always have something to say about mind control, manipulation and the government. Even though some of them take their notions to the extreme, and, therefore, sound a little crazy, there may be some cause for concern.

There is existing technology that has been developed which has the ability to infer on a person's mental state using a brain scan, and the technology goes as far as being able to see the content of one's thoughts. It is possible to implant a behavior or induce an abnormal mental state. Most of these technologies are government sponsored and should they become fully effective, they are likely to be found everywhere in the future.

One of the existing mind control programs in the United States of America is with the CIA, and it is known as Project MKUltra. It is referred to as an illegal programme which undertook a range of experiments on human beings. The aim of this program was to identify and develop some drugs and procedures that were to be applied and used in interrogations and torture. The intention had been to weaken the accused, and force them to give confessions. This program was initiated in the early 1950's.

It could be argued that people in the military and other armed forces are under mind-control programs from the government. These people are 'programmed' to follow instructions and carry out their assignments. They often do not share their opinions and do not speak until they are spoken to.

In addition to programming the soldiers, the military is also researching into creating applications that can be used for brain computer interfacing. This is basically having military equipment that can be brain activated and controlled from a remote location. This is in effect putting the man in the machine. If this technology takes off, it will mean a complete change in the way American soldiers approach combat.

Military Brain Computer Interfacing Techniques

There are three main techniques that the military are exploring in regards to mind control and BCI principles. These are explained below: -

1) Telepresence

This is the most common application of BCI technology to date, and it looks at the possibility of having a human bring operate a machine at a distance in a remote environment. What makes this machine different from other remote controlled machines is the fact that it is brain actuated and a robot.

The issues that have stopped this technology from actively being used at the moment are the fact that BCI are still a little slow, and they take high cognitive demands on the user. There are also variable communication delays that cause a serious problem.

All this may sound like it is positive and an excellentmove in development, but there are dangers that could lead to damage to the psychology of the human controlled. First of all, there is a lack of emotion that exists when operating machinery. The same decisions that would have been made will be changed. The aspect of humanity becomes lost, and the decision-making can turn cold, thoughtless and lack compassion.

In the long run, this will undoubtedly affect the capability of operation for the human controller. They may be requiredto recover still from PTSD even though now they were not physically on the battle field.

2) Robotic augmentation

This takes the man and machine union a step further than telepresence. In this technology, human strength and endurance is augmented with exoskeletons to create a stronger fighter who can make swifter decisions and have faster reactions. These exoskeletons are also said to increase the physical strength of the wearer, enabling them to punch through doors quickly. It also has the advantage of being agile so that movement is quick, and the body can quickly respond to sudden changes in the environment.

In effect, it gives a soldier the power of three soldiers. The reasons that it is not being widely used so far is the fact that it requires a permanent connection to a power supply. Until it can be self-powered, it will remain in the prototype stage.

It is intended to be used by injured soldiers, giving them a chance to go to battle despite their injuries. Sounds noble. However, the problem is that some may take this advancement in technology and use it to play God.

With the wrong soldier, this exoskeleton can be used to control people through fear and aggression. Rather than help the soldier it can mess them up by giving them a psychological complex.

In an extreme case, it may become impossible to separate the soldier from the exoskeleton.

3) Overcoming injuries

This is a move in technology that is meant to benefit those who are paraplegic. It involves giving the soldier a self-powered eLEG that runs electronically and is powered directly by the soldier. This is meant to go hand in hand with an electronic wheelchair, as well as some sort of exoskeleton.

The same problems that will be faced with Robotic augmentation may result with this technology as well. Instead of taking the time to deal with the injuries and recover psychologically from the conflict, the soldier may opt to skip psychological recovery due to the physical patching up.

The problem here is that psychological problems do not go away, and the soldier may be susceptible to fits of rage and a loss of control. This will lead to the adoption of coping mechanisms that may involve the control of others as a means to an end.

From this example, it is noted that there are the obvious mind control techniques that are used by the military to control behavior and make sure everyone is kept in life. However, there are also more subtle ways that mind control can occur, disguised as a helping hand, but possible harboring an ulterior motive.

Before these technologies are released and people allowed to use them freely, there should be some intensive research done on the possible long term effects and how they can be countered, particularly if they will suppress people or lead to suppression.

If used properly, these technologies are the way to the future, and should be embraced and promoted.

Chapter 34:
Mind Control and Persuasion

Persuasion is defined as the act of persuading or coaxing a person to do something or believe in something. When received in relation to mind control, coercive persuasion and exploitative persuasion are addressed.

Coercive Persuasion

When you are using coercive persuasion, you are making an active effort to force others to alter their beliefs, attitudes, ideas or behavior. In order for coercive persuasion to be effective, there is a need to use threat, emotional pressure, intimidation, undue influence, anxiety and stress. This type of persuasion leans to the negative side of mind control.

If you would like to experience or at least see coercive persuasion being practiced, you should view training in the military. Aggressive tones, shouting, and commands are used get militants to behave in a certain way. This also applies to terrorist organizations, cults, pushy sales based companies and even certain professional and academic institutions.

Coercive persuasion is a way to control people's minds by stopping them from making informed decisions. It trains people to rely heavily on their superiors if they want to get anything done.

Coercive persuasion strategies can be extremely subtle, or in some cases, considered the norm for moldingbehavior. The result of people who are experiencing coercive persuasion is the complete breakdown of their emotional defenses. They would be unable to think cognitively and intricately, and in some cases, even their approach to relationships and their personal conduct would be affected. These people suffer from being unable to make rational decisions or to objectively review a situation.

Coercive Persuasion Techniques

In order to defend yourself from coercive persuasion, you need to be aware of the techniques. Some of them include: -

Coercion Technique 1 – Isolation

Breaking down someone's supportive social environment is a good starting point for effective coercive persuasion. When one is away from family and friends, they lose objective minds that can offer advice. Therefore, they seek direction from authority figures as well as information. This lead to emulation of the behaviors in this new group and a person becomes dependent on acceptance as well as propaganda.

Coercion Technique 2 – Intimidation

Once people are in a group, they become easier to intimidate as a technique towards achieving mind control. Intimidation entails subtle and sometimes not so subtle threats to avoid any type of disobedience. These threats open include physical or mental harm, separation or divorce, financial ruin and so on. The end result is to get people to take up certain beliefs and attitudes, as well as to alter their behavior.

Coercion Technique 3 – Attach Self Confidence

When a person is self-confident, they are able to defend themselves, make reliable decisions and even fight for what is right in a situation. However, one their self-confidence has been undermined, the person becomes indecisive, confused and powerless. Mind control can be achieved by creating intense situations where one can repeatedly undermine another's judgement. Putting psychoactive drugs in water or food can further add to a feeling of powerlessness.

Coercion Technique 4 – Emotional Overload

There is a saying that goes 'when it rains, it pours', and certainly, there are times when life feels as though everything that could go wrong, does go wrong. At times like these, a person often experiences a short period of stress and then things begin to come together, and they are able to cope. When using coercive persuasion for mind control, a whole range of negative emotions are repeatedly heaped on a person. These would include humiliation, guilt, isolation, manipulation and loss of privilege for example. A person experiencing all these continuously would find it difficult to recover and adequately cope.

What makes coercive persuasion so successful is the complete oblivion of the victims involved. As they are wallowing in intimidation and confusion, as well as being victimized, they do not realize what is happening until they might have some time to move away from the situation, and then look back to understand why they had been so compliant.

Exploitative Persuasion

One of the factors that makes mind control so powerful is its invisibility. It seems to sneak up on you and take over all your senses. Some people can identify certain aspects of mind control, particularly coercive persuasion, and therefore they believe that they are safe from mind control entirely.

They might even go as far as to claim to be resistant to it. These are the people who are most likely going to be affected by exploitative persuasion.

In this type of manipulation, a person believes very strongly that they can never be manipulated, and when actions are put in place to manipulate them they are completely blind to them. One example of mind control using exploitative persuasion is cultivating a 'us' versus 'them' mentality. 'Us' represents a group that are enlightened and have to create a distance from 'them'.

Them are the people who do not understand and are not loyal to the truth. This type of mentality creates deep suspicion and distrust of other people and it is quite sufficient. What happens next is people choosing to isolate themselves from others.

Chapter 35:
Mind Control and Deception

When someone is being controlled or manipulate through mind control, it is very likely that there is a heightened level of deception included. The most basic type of deception here is misinformation or failure to disclose important details.

Take, for example, a group looking to recruit new members. They may be aware that the full activities within their group may be a deterrent for new members. They, therefore, choose to disclose limited information in the hope that they will convince new people to join them. In other words, they hide their true colors and intentions.

It is only when the new member is ingrained in the activities of the group that the intentions come out, and by then it might be difficult to give in or give up.

People who find that they have been deceived into mind control are often in such a situation due to circumstances in their lives. At times of crisis, it is hard to think correctly, and, therefore, people are more susceptible to being taken advantage of or believing information that goes against their core understanding.

Here are some of the things that they go through when they are being indoctrinated into a group or be a person focused on mind control.

a) **Isolation** – This requires you being separated from the people that you love, and quite often, from familiar surroundings. This is to make sure that you are not in any place that you may consider familiar.

b) Fatigue – Keeping you busy until you are too physically exhausted to interact with others or ask questions. This will make you less resistant.

c) Hunger – Avoiding the chance of giving you food or water for a long period of time. The result of this is when you are given the food or water; you are so grateful that you would be willing to do anything to get some.

d) Repetition – Telling you the same thing over and over again. This is often what happens to people who object to some information. The end result should be a lack of resistance, and you beginning to believe that the information you received was accurate.

e) Unpredictability – Ensuring that the circumstances around you are unstable so that you never know what could happen. You would be living from a state of anxiety.

Deception as a means to mind control is especially powerful, when a leader is the primary target. This deception takes place through a process called thought reform. By changing the leader, the information that the follower receives can be tailored to fit the agenda of those responsible for mind control.

There needs to be a certain atmosphere to put a system for thought reform into place. Dr. Margaret Suger established these four conditions for thought reform, on a person by a group.

1) Ensure that the person is now aware of how they are being changed. Change using thought reform needs to be subtle and done one step at a time. The person at the

helm will be looking to establish a change in the person being reformed's ideas.

2) Control a person's time, and their physical and social environment. In this condition, a person is kept busy with work for the group looking to establish control. It gets to the point that they are doing work for this group in every spare moment that they have.

3) Slowly establish a sense of powerlessness in the person. This requires isolation of the victim and surrounding the person with members of the new group. Before long, the person will have no choice by to mimic the behaviour of other group members in order to fit in.

4) Make sure that they system of rewards and punishments is manipulated to suit the groups ideology. This can be done by teaching paced speech patterns, using guided imagery and subjecting a person to lengthy lectures or meditation sessions.

If thought reform is successful, the individual will have their personality deeply affected. The physiological and psychological elements of their functioning shall be detrimentally altered.

Chapter 36:
Mind Control and Hypnosis

Hypnosis has long been seen as a method of mind control that can effectively lead to altered behavior. People have been using hypnosis when they want to lose weight, make a decision to stop smoking and even to avoid losing one's temper.

Hypnosis requires a person to move in and out of a stage of consciousness. To further understand how hypnosis affects a person through the day, it is imperative to understand the different sets so that your pastor can use them when necessary.

When considering states of consciousness, there is the waking state which is the state that you will be in when you are awake, alert and ready to face the day. Throughout the day, your states of consciousness will chance.

For example, you could enter a trance state while you are in the bath. In this state, you would be warm and comfortable, lying down and possibly wanting to take a nap. You could also experience a hypnotic trance state where you focus most of your attention on what is happening on the outside, rather than what occurs on the inside.

In his trance state, you are likely to be more aware of your surroundings, your internal dialogue by way of thoughts, internal feelings and any messages. This allows for interaction between family members.

Hypnosis is relatively easy to master, and once you understand how to execute the technique, you can do so with any person you speak to, without them realizing what is happening.

Although this may seem exciting for a person who wants to hypnotize people for their own entertainment, it is potentially dangerous when used as a mind control technique where someone has their own agenda to fulfil.

As knowledge is power, it is important to know how hypnosis is done so that you are aware when someone tries to use the technique on you.

Hypnosis during normal conversation

The first thing you need to do if you want to hypnotize someone during an ordinary conversation is to establish trust. With that, a person will lower their psychological defenses leading to them being relaxed around you.

A good way to establish trust is to mirror the other person's behavior and body language. This is known as pacing. This should not be done obviously, but requires some restraint on your part.

With a good trust base, you can then alter their strategy consciousness. Get them to talk about an experience which you know will relax them. This will fit them into a trance like state. Now you can attempt to control their minds by giving commands which have been embedded in sentences or phrases.

Take, for example, this command, "sit down there!" As they speak, you can put it into various sentences for example asking them, "Did you sit down there on Wednesday." By repeating this phrase in subtle ways, you can give them a subliminal message that makes them want to sit down there.

Effects of a hypnotic trance

When people are in a hypnotic trance, they become very suggestible to mind control techniques. What happens is that their ability to think rationally, logically and critically, begins to diminish until there is none of this behavior left. They are willing to accept any suggestions that are given to them. It is this state that most people will associate with hypnosis.

The thing to note here is that it does not matter how strong or confident a person may be when they are faced with hypnosis. Once they are in this state, they are the same as everyone else who has been in the same state.

This type of trance is also highly favored by leaders of cults because it means that their members cannot think for themselves, and, therefore, cannot object to anything that they see or are asked to do. When in this state, you can get people to violate their own moral codes and personal ethics, and in turn, to do things that they would normally never do.

People who are tired after a long day of work often feel dazed and find it difficult to concentrate or focus on a particular thought. They are in effect in a self-induced trance like state. In this state, they are particularly easy to hypnotize as they will offer little resistance, and this makes them vulnerable. They are especially susceptible to control, and it is no wonder that leaders in cults will usually use hypnotic techniques on their members after a long day's work.

Finally, one can be overwhelmed into a trance-like state from pressure given by a group. If everyone is doing the same thing, you may feel like the odd one out in a negative way if you are not also indulging in this behavior. To avoid being berated you decide to follow the crowd and possibly indulge in behavior that you would normally avoid. You are in a hypnotic state where you find yourself unable to resist what is happening around you.

Why do people use hypnosis?

The main reason that people will use hypnosis is the sense of control that they enjoy when they can make a person do whatever it is that they want. It feels powerful to be able to program and control another person. This issue of control has become a problem for most hypnotists as they enjoy the power that they have over people's actions ad lives.

Hypnotists can sometimes manipulate others into believing that they are in control of what is happening by suggesting that at the core of it all, they make the decisions about how to behave and what to do of their own volition. These give the person being hypnotized an accurate illusion of control, and the illusion that is non-existent.

People who have been hypnotized do not need to be sitting somewhere in a quiet room with the lights out in order to actually experience being hypnotized. Yu may find that you are interacting with someone who was hypnotized since they were in a trance that affected the functionality of their brain. On the surface, they may seem aware of their surroundings, of answering questions and being an active part of the conversation. A hypnotized person is there, yet they are not there at the same time.

As a method of mind control, hypnosis is very easy to use. Once you have been able to establish a trigger with someone, all you need to do is get them into a hypnotic trance. This can usually be done by saying one word or phrase which would sound completely reasonable to a person who happened to be walking or passing by.

The better a person becomes at getting people to that hypnotic trance, they more they can develop their skill so that when they want to hypnotize someone, they do not even need to use any words. They could use actions that help get a person into the relaxed trance state, such as giving a massage which results in the entire body relaxing.

Hypnosis is nothing magical or difficult to achieve. It is simply an altered state of being that allows someone to control part of a person's thinking and actions. It is meant to last for short periods of time. Therefore, it is not possible to hypnotize someone today and expect them to be in the same state a year from now.

In a day, as human beings we are coming in and out of a range of states and trances. It is important to be aware of when you are most vulnerable because it is at that time that others can easily hypnotize you without giving you a chance to mount any type of defense.

Hypnosis is a particularly dangerous form of mind control because someone can bring you into an altered state where you can be controlled without physically having any contact you, and even without saying any words. Anyone is vulnerable, regardless of how strong their personalities may be.

The most damaging thing about hypnosis is the power has to reduce all mental faculties and make someone unable to accurately evaluate information. It is unlikely that one would even realize that they are in an altered state. That is why it is important that one learns how to identify warning signs before there is a need for defense.

Chapter 37:
Mind Control and Cults

By far the most prevalent forms of mind control are those that are found in cults. This type of mind control has even spurned phrases like a "cult following" to describe the 'blind' way in which cult members hold on to their beliefs.

Cults are often ascribed to religion, but they are much more than that. A cult is basically any group or movement of people that exhibit an excessive devotion or intense dedication to a person, ideology or object. Cults will often use highly unethical and manipulative methods of control through persuasion to move forward the agenda of the group's leader. The problem with cults is that this agenda is usually to the detriment of the other members, their family units and the community at large.

Human beings have an inbuilt capacity to exploit one another. That is why it is so easy for cults to form and be maintained. Cult members are not a group of crazy people who have an irrational point of view. Cults can be made up of anyone, including the rich and poor, young and old, educated and uneducated.

Why do people change when they join cults?

People change when they join cults due to several factors. The first is that they are isolated. Following this, they start to imitate the behavior of the other cult members around them. This is because human beings have an inherent need to fit in. The cult's way of thinking, acting and feeling soon becomes second nature. Their previous personalities become suppressed and eventually reduce due to not being 'activated.'

At the beginning of the cult experience, people behave in a shell shocked manner. When questioned about anything, they will find it difficult to answer and be distance with other people. Mind control is slowly changing the person and after a while, they convince themselves that the cult is what they want, and it becomes evident that they are fully under mind control.

The mind control techniques used by cult members are subtle, often require patience but turn out to be highly effective. Deception is inherent, as cult members hide the truth until you are thoroughly embroiled in what they do. They are also likely to have excellent public relations that will provide information about all the good deeds that they are involved in, such as how they help the poor, support medical research and build up the environment.

They also support an exclusive belief system. This is essential for mind control as it is intended to discount everything else that you may know or believe. It is not enough to simply alter the belief system. To belong to a cult, a person also needs to believe that the new system can only be enforced within the cult group, and this is often a fear based mechanism for control.

Eventually, people begin to hide their real thoughts and feelings in a mind control cult, and will instead appear to wear a mask that presents them as a perfect cult member. This is to ensure that the leadership never finds out that the member is not measuring up, as this could cause some form of punishment. Under mind control, the deception goes beyond the people on the outside. It also includes delivering those within the cult.

This puts a stop to the formation of truly close relationships within the cult. A further form of mind control is to ensure that the members are so occupied with the cult's activities that they are too exhausted to interact with each other, let alone their friends and family outside of the cult.

Once a person become a full member of a cult, and their minds are being controlled, they are encouraged to get others to join the cult. The strategies that they use are known as cult recruitment techniques. Before you end up a victim of a cult, exposed to mind control, you can watch out for the following methods: -

- **Hyped up Meetings**

  Instead of sitting with you one on one to explain what their group does, they will insist that you attend a group meeting. What often happens is you arrive at the meeting and encounter a room full of very enthusiastic individuals. Even if you had reservations about the group, you might begin to wonder what is wrong with you. Peer pressure is then applied whereby you will feel uncomfortable until you join them.

- **Continuous and Unrelenting Pressure**

  The cult members need to keep you in a mind control environment until you join their cult. They do this by applying constant pressure on you until you feel you have no choice but to give in. They could accomplish this by repeatedly calling, meeting you everywhere possible as you go through your routine, and take more time than expected at meetings. All this is intended to immerse you into the cult.

- **They will insist that they are not a cult**

  Friends and family will likely see the gray areas within the group and warn you. Therefore, before this happens the group will take a pre-emptive strike and warn you about how people do not 'understand'. When it happens, you will believe that what the cult members have told you is true.

The important thing to remember about mind control techniques, used in cults is that they take time. There are several steps employed, an agenda being followed, a charismatic leader to please and a lot of false promises. Cult members are not crazy, they are unfortunate for being controlled.

Chapter 38:
Mind Control Technology

As the world evolves and begins to depend on technology, the older methods of mind control are becoming more and more irrelevant. Scientists and researchers are now looking into more technology-based methods of mind control. One of the things that have been attempted is the transmission of thoughts from one person to another through a computer.

What is supposed to happen is one person has a thought, and the other person physically excites or acts on that thought. This type of mind control takes manipulation to a whole new level. The person who is meant to act on the thoughtusually has limited to no awareness of what they are doingand, therefore, are unable to object in case they ae not comfortable with the scenario. This is a form of a human to human mind control.

Although this technology is already revealing good results, scientists are interested in getting more out of the existing technology. They are working on developing something that is able to transmit concepts and thoughts, rather than just impulses. The idea behind this is that in the future, it will be easy to transfer knowledge from a teacher to a student.

Although these plans appear to be noble and for the benefit of learning, in the wrong hands, this mind control technology can be extremely dangerous. In a sense, it is leading to 'reading of minds' and it can be used to harvest information from a person involuntarily.

Combating Terrorism with Mind Control Technology

Around the world, there are programs being created with mind control technology as a basis to combat terrorism. Unfortunately, they will impede on the privacy of people in general. The National Security Agency (NSA) in the United States of America has managed to develop efficient methods of controlling the human brain. The call the technology Remote Neural Monitoring (RNM). It is intended to bring a complete change to the way crime is detected and investigated.

This technology is able to remotely read a brain so as to detect if there are criminal thoughts taking place. These readings are carried out by supercomputers which also have the capacity to send messages through a person's nervous system so as to influence their behavior in a desired fashion. This technology has been under development for the last 50 years.

It currently is able to read and control a person's emotional processes of thought, in combination with their dreams and subconscious. Electromagnetic frequencies are used to stimulate the brain.

This technology works without there having to be any physical need with the subject. The process is as follows. An encoded signal is sent to the auditory cortex through RNM. This signal bypasses the ear, and it is meant to detect audio communication. In addition to this, it is capable of performing electrical mapping of the activity in the brain. It is able to bypass the eyes and the optic nerves by going directly to the visual center and thus projecting images from the brain to a video monitor.

The technology is able to manipulate emotions and thoughts, and also to read thoughts remotely. As a tool for mind control, it can cause severe pain to every nerve in the body, and it allows for remote manipulation of behavior. It also is able to control a person's sleep patterns, which makes communication with the sleeping party easy.

Mind Control Technology for the Military

The military in the USA is changing rapidly, with more and more people are going to be replaced by the USA. There is technology under development that is creating a brain controlled tanks, which a person can remotely operate from a base without having to put in a driver, automated attack drones and a range of mind control techniques.

Of course, this new technology will lead to a change in the approach to handling conflict. The problem with this is that the breakthrough creates a broad and detailed writing job.

Neuroscientists are now the ones making military gear.

Chapter 39:
Mind Control Myths

Now that you have an idea of what constitutes mind control, it is likely that you feel as though you can see mind control clearly for the first time. Just in case you are still working towards clarifying it in your mind, here are some myths that have existed, and which have also led to certain pre-dispositions.

Myth 1: A person being mind-controlled will behave strangely

Consider this: An individual is attending a magic show, and one of the tricks is to hypnotize a person and get them to exhibit behavior that is out of the ordinary. It may be funny to watch a person make animal sounds or jump around, but mind control does not quite work that way.

Usually, someone who is being controlled will behave in much the same way as normal. It is only if you are very close to them that you might notice some subtle changes in behavior.

Myth 2: You need to be stupid, uneducated, mentally ill, needy or spiritually weak to have your mind controlled

Mind control can happen to anyone, especially coercive persuasion. There need not be a disadvantage about a person's circumstances that makes them more susceptible. In fact, it is often very nice and kind people that fall victim to negative mind control.

People are typically more susceptible to experiencing mind control when they are facing some difficulty in their lives. This is also the case if they have a certain amount of instability. That is when they become easier to deceive. This type of mind control appears to be a solution to the problem, which makes defenses drop and opens the mind up to persuasion.

Myth 3: You need to be physically restrained during mind control

In the past, especially following the Second World War, it was believed that mind control required restraints, torture, threats and violence. However, coercive persuasion has dispelled this view of mind control. This type of persuasion requires no force whatsoever, rather, what is need is an active speaker and a receptive listener. For this persuasion to be effective, there should be an element of trust, even it if is small.

Myth 4: When under mind control, you will look glassy eyes and confused

Zombie movies have made mind control look like someone who has a complete loss of control. People being mind-controlled do not stumble around in confusion and drool. They appear to be functioning in a normal way. The reason for this is that our brains are actually primed to accept deception and manipulation tactics.

Myth 5: You can never tell you are under mind control

This is perhaps one of the reasons that mind control is as effective as most people believe that they are not being manipulated in any way. They will believe that they are in complete control of their own decisions and can, therefore, behave as they please.

However, it is possible to tell that you have been brainwashed. All you need to do us identify your triggers.

Chapter 40:
Mind Control Techniques

Now that you have read about mind control and have a clearer understanding of what it entails, you have probably identified situations in your life where you believe your mind has been controlled. For this reason, you need to equip yourself with a defense from mind control, especially negative mind control, and the best way to do so is identifying how it can be introduced to you. To accomplish this, you must learn some techniques of mind control. Knowing techniques of mind control will help you resist mind control propaganda and advertising. These methods include: -

a) **Education**: it is the most common, most obvious and also the most insidious mind control technique. This is a technique that has been in use for a very long time and it is quite popular and very useful today. If you want to influence the thinking of a large group of people, education will work out very well.

   A person is influenced the most during learning. People look up to educators to impact them with knowledge and thereby teach them how they should behave in society. While receiving an education, extremist ideas can be impaired or young minds, as well as social conditioning to promote certain behavioral in the future.

b) **Predictive programming**: predictive programming and documentaries which bring insight into what could happen in the future are a very effective way of controlling the minds of people. People who use such techniques already know what they want to achieve and so, they will try to bring out the picture of the future like something the people will totally disagree with. People who watch such programs end up doing what the programmer want, and the programmer succeeds in his game.

c) **Advertising and propaganda**:

Advertisers try to turn wants into needs, and this entails a complex change of an attitude. They do this by finding ways to target a person's self-image.

Propaganda is a tool that governments use to ensure that a particular message reaches the people. One way that governments use propaganda is by integrating a message into multiple types of information media sources. These would include print, TV, news, radio and even movies and other entertainment. In addition, subliminal messages through symbols and actions are used in this media sources. They unconsciously leave an impression in the brain and rest in the subconscious.

These are mainly not meant to create awareness but to influence people to choose one item over another especially in marketing. The main objective here is to change people's self-image so as to make them look at a need like it is a want. These days, the influence media has on people is so much and so, different bodies use the media in order to control the mind of many people.

d) **Religion, sports and politics**: these three work the same, on a divide and conquer rule. They are all effective mind control techniques. People are made to believe on one means of survival; then groups are formed in order to influence people to go for that one way so that they can survive through. In the end, they are brainwashed and made to believe something that they previously did not believe in.

e) **Drugs**: there are drugs that are used in order to make it easy for people to control the minds of others. As long as you are on the drug, you can easily be made to think like your master and do just what he asks of you. In this case, the controller has to ensure that his subject is on drugs all through for the method to work effectively. The problems with this is that the person could end up being addicted to the drug, which is not good at all.

f) **Food, air and water**: food poisons, food additives and toxins always alter the way that one's brain functions. The foods consumed these days have substances, and certain elements used in water treatment are known to alter the normal brain functioning. They leave people more prone to influence than before, which is quite dangerous. Some people can spray substances into the air in order to control the thinking capacities of other people for an individual reason.

g) **Military testing**: the military is well known for brain control in order to get unchallenged obedience from its subjects for an individual reason. This is done in the case of a dire need and the techniques used are quite safe.

h) **Nanobots**: this is a more advanced mind control technique also known as neuroengineering. It is believed to be the fastest and most efficienttechnique. It works through brain manipulation using the fiber optic.

By just a click of the button, you will have totally controlled the brain of your subject.

i) **Electromagnetic spectrum**: this is basically altering the electromagnetic field of the brain with the purpose of influencing the thinking capacity of the other person.

j) **TVs and Computers**: these are believed to affect the normal brain functioning of people. It is believed that TVs and Computers are engineered in such a manner that they can alter the alpha brain waves. That is why they affect the social life of many people who are so much into TVs and computers.

Mind Control strategies that will not fail you

So far, it is likely that you have developed some fascination for mind control. If you would like to try some techniques, here are some strategies that will help you along.

1. **Do all the thinking for the people involved.**

   If you want people to agree and do what you are asking, you will not ask them to think about it. They may not think about it the way you are doing, and this will not help with the results that you are expecting. Again, people are too busy thinking about other things and so, they may not have the time to think about what you are telling them. Think of them and give them facts about the matter and you will have influenced them. This is what marketers do all the time.

2. Start small

To succeed in mind control, you should not try to control so many people at once. Start with just a few people and once you succeed in it, take another small group of people, as you try to get the first group to try influencing a few more people. Before you know it, so many people are convinced already, and much of your work has been done.

3. Do it step by step

Ask for an inch and take a mile. You have to try influencing people bit by bit. If for instance you are trying to get them to use a certain product like in marketing, you have to give them little information at a time. Once you get their full attention, and you feel that they are slowly coming to your side, you can give them more information and they can do just what you want them to do.

4. You need a real deadline

You need a set time after which you should start seeing results. This will prompt you to go on however hard it may seem. Mind control is not easy especially if you are doing it on pretty difficult to convince people. You have to be tough to meet the deadline. A deadline will also help you evaluate yourself and how much you can do at a certain period of time.

5. Give more than what you are expecting

People will want to know what they will get from what you are selling to them. You have to give them something worth more than what you will receive. This way, they can trust you. Give them good and valid reasons why they should actually believe you and you will succeed in influencing them.

6. Be completely and utterly shameless

Shame will hinder your success especially if you are in marketing. You have to be totally shameless in order to succeed in influencing people. Be ready to talk and try to convince people shamelessly about the things that you want them to believe in. tell them the benefits and the consequences of not following what you are saying and you will succeed in it.

Mind control is safe as long as it is not used for negative or selfish reasons. Once the purpose has been achieved, you should let the person live their lives normally. It is always advisable to use positive influence in order to get positive and long term results. If you use mind control for selfish reasons, you may get unpredictable results, which could go wrong in the future once the other people realize that you have been using them all along. That is why you should give something more in order to get something back when you are at it. This way, the people will get something, and you will get what you were looking for.

Chapter 41:
Tips to avoid Mind Control

Mind control to a large degree has to do with emotional manipulation. This is what occurs when a person makes you feel bad about yourself because you do things differently from them. What often happens is you end up feeling self-conscious and want to fit into the group.

This is a powerful mind control method because you hand over all your power when you allow someone to control your emotions. If you find yourself in a situation where mind control may be used to you, try the following tips to avoid being controlled.

Tip 1: Use your imagination

When you are experiencing a scenario where someone has isolated you, learn how to meditatively visualizescenarios where you are able to interact with your loved ones. This will help you to avoid the feelings of helplessness and loneliness as well as keep you from needing too much human interaction. This would stop you from talking to the wrong person when you are seeking for help.

Tip 2: Role Play Mentally

Once you know about mind control, it becomes easier to notice. Avoid taking any drugs or medication that would impair your judgement. By noticing a mind game or a control tactic for what it is, you immediately reduce the power it can have on your being.

Tip3: Dissociate

After a while, you will have the skills in place to discern when a person is playing mind games with you so that they can cause you some humiliation. You need to create yourself an emotional defense and dissociation is an excellent option. This takes your mind and body away from the situation, almost to the point that it feels like it is happening to someone else.

Tip 4: Observe Communication

Take the timeto really listen to what is being said and the way it is being communicated. Do you feel uncomfortable and pushed to the wall, even with a calm and caring sentence? Your subconscious will alert you when the conversation seems to have a hidden agenda behind what is obviously being expressed. You should allow yourself to listen to it, and then leave the conversation.

Tip 5: Stand out

The last thing you would probably like to do is stand out from the crowd, but you may be forced to do so in order to avoid being controlled. You should be ready to disobey the stipulated social norms and rules of polite society if it will mean that you save yourself from the trap of being under someone else's control.

Tip 5: Avoid pleasing others

If you are uncomfortable with a scenario and do not want to engage in activities that seem like they will harm you, then don't. Avoid getting pushed into doing something that you do not want to do, just so that you can please other people. You do not need to make rushed decisions. You have the right to defer a decision, or even to just say no.

Tip 6: Get all the information that you need

In order to get you into a situation where you will experience mind control, it is likely that you will be given scanty information that is difficult to back up and often seems too good to be true. If you feel the need to, look for as many sources of information as possible and make sure that you are well informed before you make a final decision.

Tip 7: Keep your secrets

A person who is interested in controlling you would like to know all your secrets – those things that you have not told anyone at all. It may seem that they care and want to build a deeper relationship with you when in actual fact, they may be looking for information that they can hold against you. If someone asks you to confess to something or give intimate information, you should be wary of their intentions for you.

Tip 8: Avoid rash decisions

If someone has been working to control your mind, and you are taking too long to do what they would like, then they are likely to lose patience. At this juncture, they may try to rush you into making a decision, and you would feel guilty especially if you see their frustration and even anger towards you. This can cause you considerable stress. Avoid making decisions when you are feeling stressed, especially when you are around the person who is causing you the stress.

Tip 9: Don't allow other to make you feel guilt or fear

People that look for mind control know that the best way to get to you is by making you feel some strong emotions. Emotions life fear and guilt can disable your functionality, overwhelm your senses, and have you feeling powerless. When experiencing these feelings, your ability to think critically and reason soundly is reduced. It then becomes easier for others to influence your beliefs. If you find you are experiencing these feelings, do your best to leave the situation.

Tip 10: Playing on your freedom

If a person starts playing on your freedom, it is best to avoid them. Playing your freedom is what occurs when someone keeps telling you that you are in control and have the right to make any choice that you want from the alternatives that they have presented. They may even tell you that you have been in the dark without freedom, but with them, you will get back your freedom. This type of information should keep you away from this person.

Tip 11: Critical of your beliefs

In order to get you to cross over to a different side, someone who is trying to control your mind will be very critical of all your most treasured core beliefs. They will tell how you have been doing things wrong and how they can offer you a solution, and they will encourage you to see things from their point of view so that you can enjoy better results. You need to be able to listen to this type of criticism, and to critically make your decision to not accept the information.

Tip 12: Do not disown anyone

For mind control to be effective, it is easier if you are isolated or separated from the ones you love. This allows for love bombing, a technique where members of the group come to offer your support and fill in the gap that has been left by your family and loved ones. Always make sure that you keep your family close to you because the impact of the mind control can be reduced significantly, allowing you some ease in thinking when you are interested in leaving the group.

One cannot overstate the power that confidence has when faced with a mind control situation. If you have a strong sense of self-worth and are confident, it makes it difficult for you to believe that someone could be better than you. Therefore, there is no one you really aspire to be like because you know that you are being the best version of you that is possible.

During mind control, people will try to break down the convictions of those who display confidence. They do this by dismissing your questions, giving you generalized information and explanations, and sometimes, they will use false analogies or intense jargon. If someone chooses to communicate with you in this way, do not accept it. Insist that they communicate with you clearly and concisely so that you can get a proper understanding.

In addition, do not accept that you will understand the situation in the future. This is a mind control technique designed to suck you in, and then have you living the false hope that you will soon receive an explanation. Get all your information upfront.

The tips that have been outlined so far are particularly helpful for a person who can see a mind control situation looming.

However, what can someone who is already in a mind control situation do to leave it?

Be careful of group associations

Usually, people who are being controlled will be made into members of a group, with every other member 'supporting' them. Leaving these groups is not easy. There are three main ways that people leave these groups. The first is by being thrown out of the group or banished. The second way is by being counseled out of the group from someone outside the group. And the third way would be to leave of your own choice.

People who are thrown out of the group may find it difficult to cope, particularly if they had reached the point where their entire existence depended on the group. Rather than leave gracefully, they will try everything to get back into the group, and they are completely unaware of how deeply they have been controlled and the destruction that this can cause.

When you are counseled out of the group, it becomes easier to see where you have been mind-controlled and to receive the support that you need to leave the group. This offers an opportunity to undo the damage that was caused by the mind control and get a fresh start at life.

If you are leaving of your own choosing, it is likely that your eyes started to open, and you realized that there were some things that were not right within the group. Unfortunately, you may not identify that you have been under any form of mind control. Therefore, even when these people manage to leave, they are unlikely to seek any psychological help.

Basically, to leave a group effectively, a person would need to go through a period of deprogramming. This requires spending time with the person and providing them with facts and information that can be used as evidence to reveal the depth of the deception. This could be a real eye-opener or could completely backfire. It all depends on how deep the belief of the leader is.

In the resting period or recuperation once someone is successfully out of the group, it is important to take time to equip the person with some tools, so that they are safe from going right back and ending up in the same situation. This is done by providing information on coercive persuasion, manipulation and deception. Over time and after a considerably long process, it should be possible to dismantle the mind of all its previously held phobias.

Chapter 42:
The Future of Mind Control

Neuroscientists have been studying the brain for years to discover all its secrets. When it comes to psychology and treatment of mental diseases, they have been able to unearth and understand which neurological impulses lead to certain behaviors and disorders.

By seeking solutions and treatments for a range of disorders, neuroscientists have discovered that by stimulating the brain in certain ways, they can both predict and control an individual's behavior. They can tell whether a person id depressed and if they may make them resort to violence, all by looking at what is happening in the brain.

There are stories that have emerged about how scientists have managed to place 'hooks' in a person's brain. They do this for particular individuals and then test out a range of neurological and physical effect. Only the targeted individual is able to hear the voices of the people controlling them, and id they share this information with anyone, they are labelled as being schizophrenic. Even though thus may be viewed as an attack, with no visible attacker, an unclear motive and no rational explanation for the attack, anyone who voices a complaint is regarded as delusional.

Best Kept Secrets

It is known that some governments already possess and use this technology which is known as V2K (Voice to Skull) communication. The most common form of this technology is the use of Nano-microchips which are implanted underneath the skin. As these microchips are smaller than a strand of hair and can be inserted from a distance, a person may have one in them with no knowledge of their existence.

The microchip can carry a myriad of programs which when released into the body, can result in a form of remote torture, especially if the person does not comply. This technology can send subliminal messages to a person by speaking to their 'subconscious' thereby making them believe that they have generated these thoughts.

They can increase paranoia or repeat a phrase so open that it becomes a basis for truth, even when it has no supporting evidence. The person under attack ends up in a position where they cannot differentiate between their thoughts and those of their attacker.

There has been talk over the years about the impact that television and the media have on mind control. This debate is destined to continue in regards to mind control in the future as televisions take on new roles. Rather than being tools used to send subliminal messages to populations, they will also be used as surveillance messages to populations, they will also be used as surveillance tools. By countering how people think and behave, messages can be created to alter their natural states.

The same goes for the internet, which is moving towards a blend or reality and virtual reality. As it is, people can be easily manipulated through the internet on their computers, tablets, video games and mobile phones. The future also holds the possibility of mind controlled robots. There is already research underway that is looking at how to combine man and machine.

Fictional movies have been created to illustrate how easy it would be to control the mind if a person who had an element of being a machine with them. Perhaps, this fiction is actually based on some facts.

The Situation on the Ground

As of the end of 2014, President Barack Obama announced that there would be $100 million placed aside for a brain mapping project around the country. It is intended that the technology being researched on and developed will provide a cure for Post-Traumatic Stress Disorder. This would be of great benefit, particularly to those who are in the military when they return from seeing horrors in the field.

However, this research has been linked to something called Transcranial Magnetic Stimulation. This is a method that a person's thought patterns can be altered in order to change their religious views and control fanaticism. This is meant to underpin the War on terror. This puts an entirely new point of view on this research, as is now appears to have the ability to control a person and violate their right to free will.

This research will give neuroscientists an even more detailed look at the brain and its functionality. Considering what is already known to date, it is clear that in the wrong hands, his technology can be highly dangerous to a person's freedom – and they would never even know it.

Chapter 43
Characteristics of a Good Public Speaker

Public speaking is something that you are going to have to deal with for the rest of your life. You will have to give presentations of some sort for your whole educational life and even for some of the sports and other activities that you might be in. When you enter the workforce, you might have to do some public speaking in order to get a job, to talk to the client, or even to announce news on television. There are many different types of public speaking that are out there and there are many different situations where you might have to give a speech. Despite all of this, there are many people who find that it is difficult to give a public speech. They might be worried that they are going to look bad while they are doing it, that they will forget their lines, or they just do not like to talk in front of other people. Even if you have these fears, it is important to learn how to get over them so that you are able to perform in your role. This chapter is going to talk about some of the characteristics that come with being a good public speaker. This can help you to see if you have some of these characteristics already; if not, you will be able to develop these characteristics in order to make speech giving easier. Some of the characteristics that are present in a good public speaker include:

- Solid content—even if you do not have a natural charisma about you like some speakers do, you will be able to get the audience on your side simply by having content that is solid and valuable to the audience. You need to make sure that all of the content you present is going to add value to the lives of the audience in some way. If you have a lot of fluff, just throw that out because it will make the audience bored and they will not take you seriously.

- Humor—people will always remember a speaker who was able to make them laugh. The earlier that you are able to get the audience smiling and laughing with you the more memorable your speech is going to be. This is because it is going to help make the audience around you more receptive to the ideas that you are getting across. Having humor in your speech does not mean that you must be a comedian, just add in a few jokes and some irony and you are sure to get the audience on your side.

- Organization—before going out for a speech, you must make sure that you are completely organized. Have all of the facts checked, the information in order, and everything in its place. There is no excuse that allows you to ramble on through the presentation. This is just going to make the audience get lost or make you lose your credibility. If you are organized, you are leaving your audience with a message that they can understand and which is easy to remember.

- Approachable—the best speakers are the ones who seem like they are approachable. These are the ones who will meet and greet people before and after the speech and who will leave room for questions at some point. These are the speakers who do not seem like they are in a rush to leave right away but instead would rather spend their time with the audience.

- Authentic—people want to know who you really are; they are smart enough to know when you are trying to pull one over on them and they will become less receptive if they feel like you are doing this. They want to hear someone who is going to be honest to them. If you are a shy person, it is fine to show this out a little in the speech because it lets people know that even though this is your fear, you feel that your message is important enough to share.

- Natural—when you are up in front of an audience, you should try to act natural and calm. This will help the audience to feel like there is a connection and they will be able to listen more closely this way. It can often spell disaster if you are sitting there acting off or being too nervous. Try to act like the audience is some of your close friends and you are sharing something with them rather than worrying about a large crowd.

- Passion—a good speaker is someone who is really passionate about what they are saying. They know that their information is valuable and useful and they want to get it out to the audience. When you are excited about the message, the audience is going to catch on to that excitement and they will be excited soon as well.

Chapter 44:
Look the Part

Now that you know about some of the characteristics that you should look out for when getting ready for your next speech, it is time to learn how to look the part. Think about all of the public speaking events that you have been to in the past; what was the speaker wearing? Would a different outfit made you listen or pay attention to the speaker in a different way than you did. The way that you dress is just as important as the things that you say to the audience. Without the right outfit, no one is going to take you seriously and you will just be wasting your time.

It is never a good idea to go to a speech wearing jeans that have a lot of holes in them, a tank top, and some flip flops. This is something that would get you attention at the beach, but will probably get you in trouble with your speaking engagement. If you want to come across in a way that projects confidence and that you are a credible speaker when you are making a presentation, you need to make sure that you are dressing for the right success. In fact, there has been research done that states how 93 percent of your impact from communication is going to come from the way that you sound and the way that you look. This section is going to help you learn how to ditch those jeans and instead pick something that will work so much better for public appearance.

The first thing that you need to consider is how you are looking to the audience. Is the outfit that you wearing give you the credibility that you want, command attention and imbue you with power? Or is our outfit something that is uncertain, sloppy, and week. Would your outfit be something that is distracting from your message or is it helping you to look professional? It is important to get these questions down right away if you would like to see the right results to go with your speech.

Looking Good

Today, there are many different ways that you will be able to look good for a speech and they do not all require the traditional suit and tie like they did in the past. This does not mean that you are not able to wear a suit and a tie if you feel comfortable in these or if you feel that the message of the speech could be delivered in a better way if you were wearing this outfit. It simply means that you have a little bit more freedom to choose your speaking outfit than what was present in the past so if you are not comfortable in a suit and tie, you can make other options. Just make sure that you are always looking your best when you get up in front of the audience because there are going to be many sets of eyes that are focused on you. It is a good idea to make sure that any outfit you choose is not too snug or that you keep an extra pair of panty hose in case they get a run so that you can switch out if something happens. Make sure that all of your garments are well-fitting and clean pressed.

Another thing to keep in mind is that you should not choose an outfit based just on how good it looks, although this is important. You should also make sure to pick out an outfit that makes you feel good as well. If you are uncomfortable in an outfit, that is going to show through in the speech and can make the audience uncomfortable as well. Pick out something that looks nice and makes you feel great so that you are able to leave with some confidence.

Fabric Choice

When picking out your outfit, you should choose fabrics that are going to keep you cool and which will not show your sweat. It can get really hot when you are nervous about something so it is not a good idea to pick out fabrics that are heavy and will not breathe. You should not choose man made fabrics such as polyester since these are not going to breathe very well for you. Natural fabrics such as silk, wool, and cotton all look nice and can breathe just the way that you need them to.

Being appropriate

It does not matter how nice you think you look in an outfit, if it is not appropriate than you should not put it on for the function. You need to consider what is appropriate both for the occasion as well as for the audience at hand. Depending on the context for the speech, a floor length ball gown can be just as inappropriate as a bathing suit. What will work to wear in front of a board of directors will not always work when you are talking to a group of construction workers who are wearing flannel shirts and jeans.

One thing that you can do is wear something that is business casual and throw a jacket over. The jacket will give it more of the elegance that you will need so that you can fit into a suit and tie situation if needed, but if you find that the event is more laid back, you can take off the coat and still fit in. Another rule to remember is that the more skin that is exposed the more casual your look is. This means that a no-sleeves top will serve this principle better than short sleeves and a lot better than long sleeves. This is the same for any outfit that you might choose to wear. You can keep this in mind when determining what kind of outfit you should wear for your event.

Color

The colors that you are wearing are just as important as anything else and your audience will be taking in the color of the outfit that you are wearing as they are listening to you. Black and navy are often considered power colors, but the issue comes when most people do not look that great in them. If you do not look good in a color, it can be really distracting to the message that you are trying to get across. It is best to choose a color that compliments your eye color, hair, and skin color. Most people will be either in cool tones or in warm tones and over time you will be better able to tell which one is going to work the best for you. If you make the wrong color choices, you will either be washed out by the colors of your outfit or you are going to clash with the coloring, both of which will not work as appearance enhancers before the crowd.

One other thing that you should remember is what occurs when you wear two contrasting colors, such as black pants and a white shirt; you are basically using the colors in order to split your body into two. This is going to create an illusion of a wider and shorter figure. Most people do not like this idea and so would rather find a way to make themselves look slender and taller. To do this, you should go for a monochrome look, one that has the top matching with the bottom.

The choices that you make in clothes will make all the difference in how you feel and present your speech. If you feel good in the clothes that you are wearing, you will be able to portray that out to the audience better. It is a good idea to check ahead of your event so that you are able to determine an outfit that will go with the occasion as well as one that makes you look and feel good.

Chapter 45:
How to Practice Public Speaking

One of the best things that you can do in order to get over any nervousness that you have and to prepare of your public speaking is to practice. This might seem like something that you should not have to do; you have all of the information right in front of you and you have been spending a lot of time on the project so you feel like you are an expert on anything that has to do with this topic. While that might be true, it can be a completely different experience when you get up and actually begin talking about the subject. You might find that your notes are not enough, that you are not sure how to do transitions, that you freeze up, or that your flow is not as smooth or you need to add something else in. It is much better to find out about these things before you get up in front of a lot of people and make the mistakes. Practice at least a few times before you have to go up in front of the audience and talk to them, but if you have time to do it many times, then you should do that as well. This chapter discusses some of the tips that you should take in order to effectively practice your public speaking.

Write out your speech

One of the things that you might like trying out is to write out your speech. Get out some paper and a pen or use a computer if you think that will be easier. The writing tools do not matter as much as getting something that will be able to capture everything that you plan on saying during the speech. You should write out the introduction, then the middle, and finally the end, trying to stay as close to word for word as you are able to. Of course, when you get up and talk in front of people, you are going to change around some of the wording or say something that is a little bit different, but at least now you will have something that is written down that you will be able to practice from. You should also read through what you have written in order to find out if there are any spots that are really awkward or if there seems to be any information that is missing.

Memorize Your Speech

This one might seem like it is a little bit out there, but you should use the speech that you just wrote out and learn it all by heart. You should read off the sheet a few times to start so that you can get the pacing and the tone of voice down without having to remember all of the words. After a few times, you will feel a little more confident about what is going on and you will eventually not need to have the paper anymore. When you are practicing, find somewhere in your home or in your office that is secluded and where you will be able to be alone. This is a great way to build up the confidence that you need to give your speech and sound amazing while you are doing it.

When doing this step, you need to learn how to be natural when talking. Even though you have memorized the speech, you do not want to sound like you are just reading off the screen. Instead, pretend that you are an actor and this is your script. You need to add in some passion, something extra to get the audience's attention and make them feel like you really know what you are talking about. If you just read from memorization, the audience is going to notice and they are going to get bored really easily. The point of memorizing your speech is to give you the confidence that is needed to keep going and to not falter. You will then be able to go off the script a little bit if you need and then go back if you begin to fumble.

This is a great way to give yourself a little bit of freedom during the whole process.

Practice Speech Out Loud

It is important that you take the time to practice your speech out loud once you have it memorized. You should start from the beginning and work all the way through the body of the speech before ending with the conclusion. It is best to try and do it the same way that you would in front of the audience; if you are skipping around or just practicing one part and not the other, you might find that you are not as prepared as you would like when it comes time to talk to the audience. Also, while you are talking out loud, pretend that there are others in the room with you, even though there is not going to be anyone there. You should not only practice the words that you are going to say, but practice the inflections that will go with the words, the hand gestures, your movements, and any comedy that you plan to throw into the mix. The more that you practice all of this and put thought into it, the better it is going to come out when you are all done.

The important part about this step is that you practice as closely as you can to how you would like the speech to come out when you actually meet the audience. Everything that you practice is going to seem much more natural if you do it at least a few times before. If you spend all of your time just learning the words and nothing else, you are going to sound really stilted and hard to understand when it comes time to give the speech.

Practice without the Notes

It is important to start the presentation practice with the notes on hand. This will allow you to go through everything while just looking down if you forget something rather than going through things later and finding out that you were completely wrong. After you have had some time to practice with your notes, it is time to drop them and practice without. Ideally, you are going to have enough time before the presentation that you can learn the material and not have to keep notecards or other papers around with you. Of course, if you are only given a few days to put the whole thing together you might not have time to do this, but if you have a month or more to prepare, it is going to look more natural on stage if you are able to give your speech without any of the notes at all.

You can start this part off slowly, perhaps do each section of your speech without the notes a few times so you can get it down. After a couple of runs, you will realize that you already know the material and you do not need to have it on you in order to be successful.

Record Yourself

Once you begin to feel comfortable with your speech and everything that you are saying, it is a good idea to record yourself. First, get out a little radio recorder and have it turned on while you are saying the speech. Go through the whole speech without stopping or worrying about what you are doing. When you are done with the speech, sit down with a pen and paper and then listen to the audio recording from the beginning to the end. Do not worry too much about how the speech sounds and instead use this as a learning experience. Take down notes of what you have done wrong, spending more time on the delivery of the speech rather than if you missed some information or not. If you have a lot of ummms in your speech, figure out how you can get rid of these so that the whole thing flows together better. You will also be able to catch on to things that you thought were good to have in the speech, but now that you are hearing them played back they sound really bad or really forced. Make adjustments to your speech and then do it again with the recorder. You will find that each time you do this process, you are going to get more comfortable with the recorder and things will begin to fall into place. Continue doing this process until you think that everything sounds perfect.

After you have gotten everything to sound good on the audio recording, it is time to bring out a camcorder and do it over again. Take a video of yourself giving the speech, following the same steps as before. The point of this process is that you will now be able to see how you look to the audience. Are you twitching a lot or wringing your hands in nervousness? Do you look like you are about to fall over? You should also make sure that you are wearing the outfit that you will have on at the speech so you can see how you look with that and with your speech. Do this a couple of times until you get everything down.

These steps should be able to prepare you to give your speech in a natural way to the audience. You will have had plenty of practice with your speech and can almost recite in in your dreams. This can help you to continue on during the process without the hindrance of your notes or having to worry about forgetting important information. It can also help you to get the confidence that you need to keep on going, even if you make a mistake, and that confidence is going to radiate out to the audience and make them like you and your ideas.

Chapter 46:
Tips for Public Speaking

Here are some tips that you can take into account when you are getting ready to speak in front of an audience.

Getting Ready

- Breathe—there is nothing wrong with slowing down and taking a breath during the speech. A pause that seems really long to you is usually only a few seconds, so just breathe collect yourself and keep going when needed. It is easy to forget to breathe during the speech which can make you go through the information too fast and makes you feel really nervous. No one is going to mind if you take just a few seconds as a segue to the next point in your speech and it can help to keep the pacing.

- Make an outline—this outline can be a lifesaver if you do not have much time to prepare and are worried about getting all of the information right. Make the font a little bit bigger so that you are able to read it with a glance rather than having to concentrate too hard and lose your space.

- Own your speech—you are the expert on this topic so let others know that. They have come to you for advice; do not let your anxiety get to you. You are the expert and know what you are talking about so let that get out to the audience when you are talking to them.

While Speaking

- Eye contact—it is a good idea to maintain eye contact with the audience while you are talking. You should be able to get your energy from the audience and they are going to be able to help you a lot more if you are able to give back to them. Look your audience in the eye while you are talking to keep them focused and to help yourself look like you are in control.

- Practice to avoid nervousness—one of the best things that you will be able to do if you are nervous is to go over your speech ahead of time. You will be able to learn the material better, have something to fall back on if you forget, and will gain the confidence that you need to keep on going.

- Save questions for the end—some speakers will feel like they should have questions open at any time. They feel this will make them more approachable to the audience. This is usually a bad idea because it is going to make your ideas get jumbled and you will lose your spot. Kindly tell the audience that you will be happy to answer their questions at the end of the speech so you can effortlessly get through the material.

Avoiding Bumps

- Do not panic about the timing—when you are presenting at home, you may find that you are more calm and collected. This could result in a conflict of timing if you get nervous at the presentation and talk faster. A good way to keep track of your timing so you are not trying to rush through everything is to place your watch on the podium in front of you. Then you can see exactly how much time is left and plan accordingly.

- Watch for nervous habits—this can include things like playing with your necklace or twirling your hair. The audience will spend more time paying attention to this rather than to your speech so learn how to avoid it or do not wear any clothing or jewelry that would present the temptation.

- Bring supplies—if you are worried about getting thirsty during the speech, bring along a bottle of water. This can help avoid issues with dry mouth as well as can help you if you get stuck-no one will notice a long pause if you are taking a drink from your water. Also, some tissues in your pocket are nice if you have to sneeze or have a runny nose. Bring along a few little things that you will be able to stuff in your pockets and use if the need arises.

Conclusion

Being aware of your emotional intelligence levels allows you to branch out further and start educating yourself and practicing with the different techniques that were provided to you in this eBook. Remember that emotional intelligence has nothing to do with your IQ, but it does have everything to do with how people will perceive you and how you will feel about yourself.

Those who have a high emotional intelligence are able to be successful in their personal and business relationships because they are able to understand their spouses, children, and coworkers on a much better level. Just with a few facial expressions, we can convey whether we're sad or happy or if we're just feeling bored. When you're able to read someone's emotions, you'll be able to gauge their reaction to what you're about to say much easier. This could save you a lot of grief and hassle in the future.

So now that you have learned all about emotional intelligence and social skills, emotional intelligence and relationships, how to apply emotional intelligence, and of course, most importantly, how to develop it, the next step is to start putting it into practice in your everyday life. Emotional intelligence can help you greatly in so many situations. No matter how hard a situation may seem, with emotional intelligence it will be easier to get through. Take what you have learned from this book and use it to start living a better life today. It is not hard, and it will definitely be very rewarding!

www.ingramcontent.com/pod-product-compliance
Lightning Source LLC
Chambersburg PA
CBHW070227190526
45169CB00001B/105